Helping birth families
Services, costs and outcomes

Helping birth families
Services, costs and outcomes

Elsbeth Neil, Jeanette Cossar,
Paula Lorgelly and Julie Young

BAAF
ADOPTION
& FOSTERING

Published by British Association
for Adoption & Fostering
(BAAF)
Saffron House
3rd Floor, 6–10 Kirby Street
London EC1N 8TS
www.baaf.org.uk

Charity registration 275689 (England and Wales)
and SC039337 (Scotland)

British Library Cataloguing in Publication Data
A catalogue record for this book is available
from the British Library

ISBN 978 1 905664 95 5

Editorial project management by Shaila Shah, BAAF Publications
Designed by Helen Joubert Designs
Typeset by Avon DataSet Ltd, Bidford on Avon
Printed in Great Britain by TJ International
Trade distribution by Turnaround Publisher Services,
Unit 3, Olympia Trading Estate, Coburg Road,
London N22 6TZ

BAAF is the leading UK-wide membership
organisation for all those concerned with
adoption, fostering and child care issues.

Contents

List of tables

Acknowledgements

This study could not have been completed without the large number of people outside of the immediate research team who generously gave their help, support and expertise. We are very grateful to the former Department for Children, Schools and Families for sponsoring this study and, in particular, Caroline Thomas, for her continued patience and support. The views expressed in the research are, however, those of the authors.

We would like to thank colleagues at the Centre for Research on the Child and Family: Jo Connolly, Michelle Cooper, Nick Healey and Dr Clive Sellick, who all participated as team members at some point in the process, and many other academic and administrative colleagues at the UEA who assisted and supported us along the way. Thanks also to our PhD student John Clifton who helped with some of the coding.

We are also indebted to our research advisory group, whose members enabled us to benefit from their invaluable wisdom and advice throughout the course of the project: Jennifer Castle, Lyndsay Davison, Jenny Gwilt, Isabella Craig, Julie Selwyn, John Simmonds, Chris Smith, Carol Vella and Doreen Ward. Additionally, we are grateful for comments and support from our academic colleagues overseas: Prof. Harold Grotevant (on project design and quantitative measures), Dr Lynn von Korff (on statistical analysis) and Marta Reinoso Bernuz (on "coping with adoption").

Special thanks must also go to our team of service user consultants who gave considerable time providing invaluable feedback and suggestions based on their own personal experiences at many points throughout the study: Zoe Boreham, Claire, Anne Cooper, Imogen Cooper, Nina De'ath, Ian Eskriett, Zoë Eskriett, Geoff, Becky Hawthorn, Bernadette James, Kiri Joseph, Roma Meah, Rachel Taylor and Tracey. Thanks also to Alison Flack and Doreen Ward, who were extremely helpful in giving us advice on involving service users in research and in facilitating the meetings with these consultants.

We are also grateful to Martin Howard, who took on board our service user consultants' suggestions and helped us design effective recruitment leaflets, and to Nicole Hamilton, who helped in the presentation of the final manuscript.

Our thanks must also go to those who, for reasons of confidentiality, cannot be named: the many people in the local authorities and adoption agencies who were prepared to participate in and support this study despite the demands on their already pressurised time. We would particularly like to thank the social workers and administrative assistants who helped us with recruitment and completed our questionnaires.

Most of all, we would like to thank the birth relatives who took part in our interviews. Without their willingness to share their own personal stories, emotions and vulnerabilities, this report could not have been written. We sincerely hope that this report does justice to their experience and feelings.

Notes about the authors

Elsbeth Neil (BSc., MA, Dip.Sw., PhD) is a senior lecturer in social work at the University of East Anglia, Norwich. Her research career began in 1996 when she began a longitudinal study of children having contact after adoption. She has directed the "Helping birth families" study and its sister project exploring support for direct contact after adoption (also part of the Adoption Research Initiative and due to be published by BAAF). She is the author of several journal articles and book chapters in these two fields, including the BAAF book (co-edited with David Howe) *Contact in Adoption and Permanent Foster Care: Theory, research and practice* (2004) and *International Advances in Adoption Research for Practice* (co-edited with Gretchen Wrobel, Wiley, 2009). Elsbeth can be contacted by e-mail at e.neil@uea.ac.uk.

Jeanette Cossar (BA, MA, Dip.SW.) is a lecturer in social work at the University of East Anglia, Norwich. In addition to her contributions to the "Helping birth families" project, Jeanette has worked on the parallel UEA project looking at support for direct contact after adoption. Her other research interests and experiences are in relation to children's views of the child protection process, and the experiences of gay and lesbian young people in care.

Paula Lorgelly (BSc, PhD) has been working at the Centre for Health Economics at Monash University in Melbourne, Australia, since January 2010. Prior to this, she has held academic posts in the UK at Nottingham, Glasgow, and at UEA. Paula's research interests are varied, but generally centre on the methodological issues of economic evaluations. Paula directed the economic evaluation aspect of the "Helping birth families" study.

Julie Young (BA, PGCE) is a senior research associate at the University of East Anglia, Norwich. After several years of experience in the fields of education and counselling, she joined the UEA in 2001 to work on the "Contact after adoption" study. She has co-authored book chapters with Elsbeth Neil on the topic of post-adoption contact, including a chapter in *The Child Placement Handbook* (Schofield and Simmonds (eds) BAAF, 2009). As well as her role as a key researcher on the "Helping birth families" study, Julie has worked on a range of projects at UEA exploring the experiences of parents involved with children's services.

The Adoption Research Initiative

This series brings together the research studies in the Adoption Research Initiative (ARI), a programme of research on adoption funded by the former Department for Children, Schools and Families (DCSF). It is designed to evaluate the impact of the Government's adoption project, including the Adoption and Children Act 2002 and various related policy initiatives. The research initiative is examining how these objectives are being translated into local policies, procedures and practice.

There are seven studies within the Adoption Research Initiative. They address four broad themes: permanency planning and professional decision-making; linking and matching; adoption support; and the costs of adoption. They also complement other recently-reported and current research on the full range of placements for looked after children, including kinship care, foster care, residential care, private fostering and return home.

More information on the Adoption Research Initiative is available on www.adoptionresearchinitiative.org.uk.

Published by BAAF:
- *Enhancing Adoptive Parenting: A test of effectiveness*, Alan Rushton and Elizabeth Monck, 2009
- *Linking and Matching: A survey of adoption agency practice in England and Wales*, Cherilyn Dance, Danielle Ouwejan, Jennifer Beecham and Elaine Farmer, 2010
- *Pathways to Permanence for Black, Asian and Mixed Ethnicity Children*, Julie Selwyn, David Quinton, Perlita Harris, Dinithi Wijedasa, Shameem Nawaz and Marsha Wood, 2010

Executive summary

Aims of this study

This study set out to learn more about the practice of supporting the birth relatives of adopted children. It was commissioned by the former Department for Children, Schools and Families (DCSF), as part of the Adoption Research Initiative (ARI) studies, to explore issues relating to the implementation of the Adoption and Children Act 2002 in England and Wales. This Act contained important changes in the provision of support services for birth relatives of adopted children, recognising the lifelong impact of adoption upon them. It acknowledged a number of support needs that birth relatives may have, including: an independent worker from the time that adoption becomes the plan for the child; help in understanding the adoption process; a range of support services at different times; and for involvement in processes relating to the child such as planning contact and reports to the adoption panel. Underpinning all these services is a value base, that birth relatives are entitled to be treated 'fairly, openly and with respect throughout the adoption process' (Department of Health, 2001, p 23).

At an earlier stage of this research project, a survey was carried out which mapped services to support birth relatives (Sellick, 2007; Cossar and Neil, 2009). This found that the independent sector (adoption support agencies and voluntary adoption agencies) had a very active involvement in this area of post-adoption support – only 11 per cent of local authorities did *not* work with any independent agencies in providing services. The low take-up of support services by birth relatives was identified by many agencies.

Building on the mapping survey, this second stage of the study aimed to address five key questions:

- How many birth relatives are referred for support services and how many take up the services?
- What are birth relatives' experiences of adoption and how are they affected by the experience?

1

- What types of support do birth relatives report using and what are their experiences of these?
- How much do support services cost?
- What is the impact of support services on birth relatives?

Study design

This study was conducted in collaboration with eight agencies: one voluntary adoption agency; three local authorities; and four adoption support agencies. The study used both qualitative and quantitative methods. The research involved three strands.

The service take-up survey: Participating agencies provided information about every new person referred to their service over a six-month period (the sample size was 495). One year later, agencies then provided information about whether or not these birth relatives, who had been referred to them, had used their services. These data were used to look at the take-up of services in general and between agencies and to explore whether the take-up of services differed according to referral route, birth relative type, or ethnicity of the birth relative.

The intensive study: We interviewed 73 birth relatives (44 birth mothers, 19 birth fathers, 10 birth grandparents) and asked them to complete a mental health questionnaire. We then followed up these birth relatives approximately 15 months later, and 57 people (78%) took part at the second stage. In most cases, we interviewed people very soon after the adoption or in the midst of the adoption process. Eighty-nine per cent of our sample was white and 11 per cent of minority ethnicity. We used qualitative methods to look at people's experiences of adoption and their experiences of using (or not using) adoption support services. Our analysis focused on looking at three key outcomes: satisfaction with support services, coping with adoption, and mental health. We looked at how these outcomes related to the services birth relatives reported they had received and to the costs of services.

The economic analysis: The economic analysis aimed to estimate the cost of providing support services to birth relatives over a 12-month period. In order to do so, case workers firstly completed diaries to ascertain the amount of time spent on each of the various services provided to birth relatives. From these, the monetary cost of providing different types of support was estimated by using published unit costs. Secondly, agencies provided information about the number and type of services that each birth relative in the interview sample was provided with over one year. The costs of support services were combined with individuals' use of support services to calculate individual costs for individual service users at 2007 rates.

Findings

The referral and take-up survey

Just over half (56%) of birth relatives referred for support had used at least one session of support in the 12-month follow-up period. The two biggest referral sources were children's services (just over half of referrals came from this source) and the birth relative themselves (just over one-third self-referred). Referral routes were significantly associated with take-up of services. Of those who referred themselves or who were referred by people other than children's services, 80 per cent took up services. In contrast, only 57 per cent of those referred by children's services used services. The take-up of services varied dramatically between agencies from a minimum of 19 per cent to a maximum of 74 per cent. These differences seemed to be related to both the different experiences and expertise of agencies in achieving good take-up, and to the referral routes into these agencies.

There were no significant differences in take-up of services between birth relatives who were white and those of minority ethnicity. Two-thirds of those referred for support services were birth mothers (67%), less than 20 per cent were birth fathers (19.5%), and "other" birth relatives (the largest group were siblings, and the second largest grandparents) made up the remaining 13 per cent. Birth fathers were less likely to have taken up services than were other birth relatives.

Birth relatives' experiences of compulsory adoption

Birth relatives described multiple and long-standing problems (such as relationship difficulties, mental health problems, and substance misuse) that they felt had contributed to their children's entry into care and

3

subsequent adoption. The majority of birth relatives described the adoption process as an unfair, hostile and alienating experience and one in which they had very little power to influence events. Birth relatives' needs for support varied in relation to different stages of the adoption process. The need for support from the point at which the child enters care was apparent, as for many people this precipitated a crisis of anger, stress, confusion, and self-destructive behaviours. As the plan for adoption progressed, the need for advice and information and involvement in key decision-making stages was indicated. Once children were placed with adoptive parents, the birth relatives then needed information about the child's welfare and support to participate constructively in post-adoption contact plans.

Birth relatives' experiences of using support services

Two-thirds (66%) of birth relatives in our sample had used birth relative support services, in almost all cases provided by independent agencies. From people's accounts of the support they received, five different types of support activity were identified:

- emotional support;
- advice and information and the provision of practical support;
- help with contact;
- advocacy and liaison;
- group or peer support.

The most common type of support people received was emotional support (83%) and the least common was group support (33%). Birth relatives' levels of satisfaction with support services were very high: 73 per cent of people were primarily positive, 21 per cent were mixed or neutral and only six per cent were primarily negative. Three themes relating to satisfaction with services were identified: firstly, the *personal qualities of the worker* were important; secondly, the *confidentiality and independence* of the service on offer was vital to birth relatives; thirdly, services that were both *flexible and proactive* were appreciated.

One-third of birth relatives in the sample had not used adoption support services, and most of these had unmet needs. Reasons why people did not take up services included feeling that nothing could be done to help them, feelings of depression and passivity, resistance to engaging in emotion-focused work, and a lack of active follow-up from the agency. Many birth relatives described having very few sources of support to help them deal with the adoption. The isolation of many people from their friends and family was often evident. Surprisingly (given the hostility that many people expressed), local authority social workers in post-adoption and contact support teams were mentioned more than any other group as providing help.

Coping with adoption

Starting with a qualitative analysis of data, three dimensions of coping with adoption were identified. The first dimension was accepting dual connection: birth parents needed to understand their change in role, from being the legal parent to having no legal relationship with their child, and from being or expecting to be a psychological parent, to having someone else take over this role. Birth relatives were rated on a five-point scale in terms of how well they were coping with this dimension. The second dimension of coping with adoption was people's feelings about the outcome of the adoption for the child. Birth relatives were rated on a three-point scale as positive, mixed or negative in terms of their confidence about the outcomes of adoption for the child. The third dimension was dealing with the impact of adoption on self. This included how birth relatives felt about themselves in relation to the adoption, how well they coped with negative emotions, how well they were able to get on with their lives, and their ability to take positive actions to help themselves. Birth relatives were rated on a three point scale as positive, mixed, or negative in terms of their ability to deal with the impact of adoption on self.

Scores from the three dimensions were combined so that birth relatives had one overall score indicating how they were coping with adoption. Birth relatives' scores varied from very high to very low.

The mental health of birth relatives

We used the Brief Symptom Inventory (BSI) to assess people's mental health. The BSI looks at nine symptom dimensions, including depression, anxiety, hostility, and paranoid ideation. Birth relatives completed this measure at the same time as the first and second interviews. At both points in time, birth relatives were evidencing exceptionally high levels of psychological distress even compared to a psychiatric out-patient comparison sample: three-quarters were experiencing psychological distress at clinically significant levels. This fits with what birth relatives told us, both about their pre-existing mental health problems and their reports about the anger, anxiety, sadness, and paranoia that they felt in response to the loss of their child. These results indicate the level of need for services that birth relatives have, but also the difficulties that might impede people from receiving them.

The costs of providing support services
Support services to a birth relative (on average) were estimated to cost £511 over the 12-month study period (the range was £0–£4,563), and birth relatives were estimated to have used 8.35 support services during this period. These figures include birth relatives who used no services. The agency reported use of services by birth relatives in the study corresponded, though not exactly, with birth relatives' own reports of their service use. The costs of supporting birth relatives varied significantly between agencies, possibly indicating both different take-up rates and different levels of service provision. The cost predictions are likely to underestimate the true cost of providing birth relative support services, as recent research suggests that one component of the cost – overheads – has been traditionally undervalued in the standard costing literature.

Costs and resource use, self-reported service use, and the outcomes of support for birth relatives
For almost all the outcomes we studied, people using services (or using more services) seemed to be somewhat better off than people not using them (or using fewer services). There was some evidence that support services were having a positive impact on those people using them. Improvement in mental health over time was significantly related to resource use and cost, and people who had used services were coping significantly better than those who had not.

The provision of a greater number of different types of support

6

activities was related to satisfaction, and to higher levels of coping with the adoption. Emotional support and advice and information were associated with service user satisfaction.

Many analyses yielded no statistically significant results. This may be because of the severity, complexity and longevity of people's problems and the brevity of the follow-up, and because sample sizes were small. It is also likely that outcomes, such as people's mental health and coping with adoption, are affected by a broad range of factors, not solely by the support they received from the agency.

Summary of key findings

- The costs of supporting birth relatives were modest. Generally, the methods of intervention being employed in the participating agencies were not "specialist" in terms of therapeutic models of intervention, but they were specialist in terms of aiming to address people's adoption-related needs.

- For birth relatives who used adoption support services, the services were experienced as being helpful by the majority, and some improvement in outcomes for those using services was evident. Positive outcomes for birth relatives are likely to contribute to the achievement of positive outcomes for adopted children, as birth relatives remain a part of the child's adoption kinship network.

- For this particular group of service users, the model of service delivery that seemed most appropriate was one that is flexible, offering a range of types of support so that different individual needs can be met.

- The take-up of services by birth relatives was a problem; this is a hard-to-reach group and outreach models of service delivery seem appropriate.

- There is a need for collaborative working between children's services and independent support providers, and between both of these agencies and adult care services, to ensure that as many of those who need services are referred for help.

- Although the majority of local authorities were working with the independent sector to provide birth relative support services, it is clear from this study that there is much that children's services themselves can do (and are doing) to support and promote the welfare of birth relatives. Key areas include working in partnership through the adoption process, and ongoing support for contact after the adoption.

- Adult care service providers (for example, mental health services, substance misuse services, learning disability services) are an important part of the spectrum of care for the birth relatives of adopted children, and the better these service providers can understand the impact of adoption on birth relatives, the greater their usefulness is likely to be.

- The needs of grandparents and birth fathers appeared just as great as those of birth mothers, but these needs may be overlooked. Fathers were less likely to take up services and use them regularly compared to mothers, but without the provision of services they are vulnerable to poor outcomes.

1 The policy context and literature review

This chapter explores the legal and policy context of the research project and reviews the literature that informs this field of study.

The current legal and policy context

The Adoption and Children Act 2002 was the first substantial reform in adoption law in England and Wales since 1976. It was designed to recognise the vast changes in the nature of adoption practice that had taken place since the 1980s, in particular, the much increased use of adoption as a permanency option for older children in public care (Ball, 2005). The Act aimed to emphasise the welfare of the child throughout his or her life, to expedite decision making in adoption, and to avoid delay. The Act, implemented fully at the end of December 2005, was broad in scope, dealing with such issues as the principles and issues a court must consider when making an adoption order, making the child's welfare the paramount consideration in these deliberations; the legal process of placement and the issue of dispensing with parental consent; the regulation of inter-country adoption; the eligibility of prospective adoptive parents; birth relatives' access to information about the adopted child; and the provision of adoption support services. Of particular relevance to the current research, the implementation of the Adoption and Children Act 2002 increased birth relatives' rights to support services when their children are adopted. The legislative framework governing the process of adoption provides the legal context for birth relatives' subjective experience of their child's adoption. Before discussing legislation relating to the provision of adoption support services, changes to the adoption process are briefly outlined.

The legal process of adoption

Birth relatives in non-consenting adoptions negotiate a complicated journey governed by the Children Act 1989 and adoption legislation including the Adoption Act 1976 and Adoption and Children Act 2002. Prior to the implementation of the Adoption and Children Act in December 2005, children would be made subject to a care order and might then be freed for adoption before an adoption order was finally sought. The protracted legal process involved the progressive limiting of parental rights, where deemed necessary, to protect the child. A care order can be made only on the grounds that the child had been, or was likely to be, significantly harmed, and that this harm was attributable to the care given by the parents (s.31, Children Act 1989). A care order gave the local authority the right to remove the child from home and decide where he or she should live. Whilst parents retained parental responsibility, the local authority could limit their ability to exercise it. Parental responsibility ceased if the child was freed for adoption (s.18, Adoption Act 1976) and birth parents would not be party to any subsequent adoption application. The perceived advantages of freeing were to avoid contested adoption hearings and reduce anxiety for prospective adopters (Brammer, 2003). Birth parents could apply to revoke the freeing order if the child was not placed within a year. However, a freed child who was not placed for adoption could be left in limbo with only the local authority holding parental responsibility. Under these circumstances, the birth relative might also be left in limbo, and be provided with little information as to the welfare of their child (Murch *et al*, 1993). Direct contact with the birth relative might be reduced and then stopped, with the birth relative unclear as to when any post-adoption contact would begin. The practice of contact being terminated to allow the child to settle, combined with a lack of information about the child's welfare, could result in a period of uncertainty which did not help the birth relative in managing the emotional demands of writing to their adopted child once post-adoption contact commenced. The majority of the birth relatives interviewed in the current research have children who were adopted under the arrangements prior to the implementation of the Adoption and Children Act in 2005.

The Adoption and Children Act 2002 abolished freeing orders and introduced placement orders, which authorise an adoption agency to place a child for adoption. Under this Act, agencies can place children for adoption with the consent of each parent or by means of a placement order. The placement order route can only be used for children who are already subject to a care order or where the court is satisfied that the conditions in section 31 (2) of the Children Act 1989 are met, or if the child has no parent or guardian. In addition, the placement order cannot be made unless each parent or guardian gives their consent or the conditions for dispensing with parental consent have been met. The grounds for removing parental consent under the 2002 Act are that the child's welfare requires this (ACA 2002, s.51 (1) (b)) and the question of parental consent is decided at the placement order stage. "Parents", under the terms of this Act, means biological parents who have parental responsibility. In other words, the consent of unmarried fathers who do not have parental responsibility is not required, although the views of such fathers should be obtained. However, the Act did make an important change in respect of unmarried fathers, which is that if such fathers are named on the child's birth certificate then they do acquire parental responsibility (2002 Act, s.111). This came into force on 1 December 2003 and cannot be applied retrospectively (Ball, 2005).

Once the child is placed, parental responsibility is held jointly by the prospective adopters, the adoption agency and the birth parents. Thus, unlike under freeing orders, the birth parents retain their parental responsibility under a placement order, although their ability to exercise it is at the discretion of the local authority and in practice is likely to be significantly curtailed. Parents with parental responsibility are parties to adoption proceedings, although they may not oppose the making of an adoption order without leave from the court. Importantly, the court may make directions for contact under a placement order (ACA 2002, ss.26 and 27). Birth relatives can apply for contact with a child subject to a placement order. Any provisions made come to an end when the adoption order is made, at which point applications for contact would be dealt with under section 8 of the Children Act 1989. Whilst section 26 orders cease at the point that an adoption order is granted, they ensure the continued involvement of the court in the period between placement order and adoption and thus may influence the search for adoptive parents, contact during the early stages of placement, and possibly contact plans after the making of an adoption order. Potentially, therefore, the Adoption and Children Act may provide more clarity about arrangements for contact during the transitional phase between a care order and an adoption order.

However, it remains to be seen how the courts exercise their powers.

A recent Appeal Court judgement (Re P (A Child) [2008] EWCA Civ 535) included guidance on this question and that of post-adoption contact. It concerned a case where it was considered vital for two siblings to have continued direct contact. The court considered it essential to make section 26 orders concerning contact for the period that the placement order was in force. With regard to post-adoption contact, the judgement included a summary of preceding case law, concluding that it has been rare to impose contact orders on prospective adopters, as enforced contact is unlikely to be in the best interests of the child. However, in relation to the case in question, the Appeal Court concluded that:

> *In our judgment the question of contact between D and S, and between the children and their parents, should henceforth be a matter for the court, not for the local authority, or the local authority in agreement with prospective adopters.* (Para. 147)

Justice Wall summed up as follows:

> *We do not know if our views on contact on the facts of this particular case presage a general sea change in post-adoption contact overall. It seems to us, however, that the stakes in the present case are sufficiently high to make it appropriate for the court to retain control over the question of the children's welfare throughout their respective lives under sections 1, 26, 27 and 46(6) of the 2002 Act; and, if necessary, to make orders for contact post-adoption in accordance with section 26 of the 2002 Act, under section 8 of the 1989 Act. This is what Parliament has enacted. In section 46(6) of the 2002 Act, Parliament has specifically directed the court to consider post-adoption contact, and in section 26(5) Parliament has specifically envisaged an application for contact being heard at the same time as an adoption order is applied for. All this leads us to the view that the 2002 Act envisages the court exercising its powers to make contact orders post adoption, where such orders are in the interests of the child concerned.* (Para. 154)

This judgement provides an interesting benchmark in case law, although it remains to be seen how courts will adjudicate in the future.

The legal processes leading to adoption have been described because of their relevance to the subjective experience of birth relatives. The context in which birth parents lose their child is a complex, multi-stage legal process, the details of which surely must be difficult to fully grasp for the non-expert. Within this legal arena, parents have to hear in court that they have significantly harmed their child (or that they are likely to do so) and that, in order to safeguard their child, their own wishes and feelings must be overruled. In other words, from the point of view of parents, the legal process of adoption may be seen primarily as one that strips them of their right to bring up their child on the grounds that they have failed in their role as a parent, and deems that their child would be better off without them.

As well as changes to the adoption process, the Adoption and Children Act 2002 has introduced important changes governing the provision of adoption support services for birth relatives, as discussed below.

Adoption support for birth relatives

The Adoption and Children Act 2002 requires that the local authority should maintain adoption support services for birth parents (s.3 (1)) and should assess birth relatives' needs for adoption support services on request (s.4 (1)). However, there is no requirement that they should provide services specified in the assessment. The National Adoption Standards for England which accompany the Act state: 'Birth parents and birth families (including grandparents, brothers, sisters and others who are significant to the child) are entitled to services that recognise the lifelong implications of adoption. They will be treated fairly, openly and with respect throughout the adoption process' (Department of Health, 2001, p 23). More specific provisions in these standards include that birth relatives:

- should be helped to understand the adoption process, the legal process and their rights;
- should be entitled to have access to a worker independent of the child's social worker from the time adoption is identified as the plan for the child;

- should have access to a range of support services both before and after adoption;
- should be able to comment on reports to adoption panel;
- should be involved in discussions about contact plans and supported to fulfil them. (Department of Health, 2001, p 23)

The Adoption National Minimum Standards, against which agencies are inspected, also discusses the new provisions in relation to birth relative support in standards 7, 8 and 9 (Department of Health and Welsh Assembly Government, 2003).

Since the implementation of the Act, few studies have looked systematically at the provision of adoption support services to birth relatives, and those which do exist are reviewed later.

Birth relatives' experiences of adoption

The impact of adoption on birth relatives has long been recognised, although most of what is known about the birth relatives of adopted children relates to a very different population of people to those whose children are adopted today. Almost all research has been carried out on mothers who relinquished their children for adoption. The research on relatives other than mothers, and on the experiences of people who did not choose to have their child adopted, is very limited. This section considers the research relating to birth relatives who relinquished their children for adoption, birth relatives whose children who are in long-term care, and non-consenting birth relatives whose children have been removed by the courts and placed for adoption.

The experience of relinquishing birth relatives

Relinquishing a child for adoption is an experience of loss that can have long-term negative psychological consequences. A number of studies of relinquishing birth mothers have found that having a child adopted is an experience of loss and grief that persists beyond the immediate aftermath of the parting, and in many cases is long term. Winkler and Van Keppel (1984) studied 213 women who had all relinquished a child for adoption when they were young and single. A great sense of loss was a key feature of many women's stories and the greater the sense of loss reported by the women, the worse was their adjustment. For many women this sense of loss did not diminish with time; in fact, 48 per cent of the sample reported that it had intensified and was worse at particular times such as birthdays and Mother's Day. For some women a strong sense of loss had persisted for up to 30 years. The lack of information about the child following adoption added to the difficulties of dealing with and accepting the loss of the child. For example, one birth mother said:

> The feeling of loss has been strong for 18 years – it was as though she had died only worse, she was out there somewhere. I don't even have a right to wonder or ask how she is. Well, law or no law, I do wonder, cry and ask. (Winkler and Van Keppel, 1984, p 54)

Well over half of respondents rated the adoption of their child as the most stressful experience of their life. The psychological functioning of the birth mothers was also measured and was found to be significantly worse than a matched sample of women who had not had a child adopted. This research clearly showed that it is unrealistic to make the assumption that women whose children are adopted will quickly "get over" this experience. In many cases, the negative consequences are serious and long-lasting.

Logan (1996) looked at the mental health of birth mothers and found that many of them reported intermittent depression linked to feelings of guilt, anger, sadness and grief. In her sample, one-third of women had been referred for specialist psychiatric treatment. Many similar findings have been outlined by other researchers, both in this country (e.g. Bouchier et al, 1991; Howe et al, 1992; Wells, 1994) and abroad (e.g. Deykin et al, 1984; Condon, 1986; Rockel and Ryburn, 1988) and key themes are obvious in biographical accounts (e.g. Powell and Warren, 1997). Research suggests that birth mothers experience a complex grief reaction including feelings of anger, loss, guilt and low self-esteem, which often intensifies over time and has an impact on subsequent relationships.

For many birth mothers who relinquished their children (most notably in the period from the Second World War to the 1970s), the decision to relinquish was made in the context of a social climate where the stigma of illegitimacy was immense and the support for single parenthood minimal. The adoption process was experienced by many as being both coercive and shameful (Kelly, 2009). In such cases, the word "relinquishment" somewhat obscures the involuntary nature of these placements; in reality, some birth mothers in the past will have had little more choice in the adoption of their child than contemporary birth parents who lose their child through court proceedings. Within such a stigmatised social climate, the loss of a child to adoption is further compounded by negative societal reactions and a consequent shortage of social support. Howe *et al* (1992) discussed the plight of birth mothers with reference to the concept of "spoiled identity" (Goffman, 1963). They argued that women who have had a child adopted are "discreditable": they have transgressed rules regarding sex outside of marriage and further have failed as mothers by giving their child away. These aspects of their identity are not immediately apparent but if they were to become known, the woman faces censure. The stigma may partly explain why some women were told by professionals and family alike to forget about the experience and put it behind them (Powell and Warren, 1997). The concept of a spoiled identity is also very helpful when thinking about relatives whose children are adopted from care, as they have failed to live up to society's definition of good parents.

There has been a massive decline in the number of women relinquishing babies for adoption, but some women do plan adoption for their child as a positive choice. For example, in a longitudinal study undertaken in the USA, 76 per cent of birth mothers said that their main motivation for relinquishment was that they did not feel ready to parent the child (Henney *et al*, 2007). Many mothers believed that adoptive parents could offer their child a more stable and secure family life. The mothers in the study experienced a range of openness arrangements, unlike many mothers in previous studies where the adoption was almost invariably closed. The research team looked at birth mothers' grief in relation to the adoption 12 to 20 years after placement (Henney *et al*, 2007). They found that 13.4 per cent of mothers were still experiencing a strong degree of grief and loss and 59 per cent reported some or a moderate degree of ongoing grief. Just over a quarter of the sample (27.6%) reported no current feelings of grief, suggesting that a positive resolution of painful feelings is possible in some cases. No one type of openness was found to be best for all birth mothers, but mothers who had the least contact were the least satisfied with their openness level, and those who had the most contact were the most satisfied (Henney *et al*, 2004). This research suggests that, where birth mothers have a measure of choice over whether to place their child and under what openness arrangements, long-term negative consequences of adoption need not be inevitable.

There is a very limited amount of research into the experiences of birth fathers; only three significant studies have been undertaken (Deykin *et al*, 1988; Cicchini, 1993; Clapton, 2003). These studies all suggest that many birth fathers also experience long-term negative consequences as a result of their child's adoption, particularly in situations where they had no choice or control over the adoption. Fathers have been found to experience a similar range of emotions to birth mothers, including sadness, guilt, frustration, emptiness, confusion and inadequacy, which did not lessen over time (Clapton, 2003). Relatives other than birth parents have also received scant attention. Some experiences of grandparents have been described (Tingle, 1994; 1995) and these descriptions indicate that having a grandchild adopted can also be desperately painful.

Birth relatives' experiences in non-consenting adoptions

Most children adopted today in the UK are removed from their parents using compulsory legal powers and are adopted without the consent of their birth family. The research on the psychological impact of this type of adoption is virtually nonexistent. Because of this paucity, it is necessary to look at the experiences of parents of children in the care system. The responses of relatives of children in care suggest that the non-consenting nature of the loss may make resolution particularly problematic. One such project is a longitudinal study of the parents of 360 children in foster care, carried out in the USA (Jenkins and Norman, 1972). The situations of these parents were in many ways similar to the difficulties of the parents of children adopted from care. Jenkins and Norman called the feelings of parents about their separation from their child "filial deprivation" and they described the most common feelings as being sadness, worry, nervousness and emptiness. Mothers whose children had been compulsorily removed were significantly more angry and nervous than were other mothers. As with relinquishing parents, in many cases painful feelings did not reduce over time. Many of these themes are echoed in the UK studies of Aldgate (1980), Thorpe (1980), Rowe *et al* (1984), Millham *et al* (1986), Lindley (1994) and Masson *et al* (1997). Millham *et al* (1986) followed an intensive sample of 30 families and interviewed birth parents. They emphasised the sense of violation that parents feel when children are removed from home. Mothers were described as experiencing 'a deep sense of failure in a role that society holds in high esteem' (p 225). O'Neill (2003), who conducted research in Australia with parents whose children had been removed by the child protection system, pointed out that birth parents may be isolated in terms of their family and community support networks. This may have contributed to why their child was removed and would certainly contribute to their ability to cope subsequently. A recent study of the experiences of parents, whose children are in long-term foster care (Schofield, Ward and Young, 2009), uses the concept of cognitive dissonance to understand how parents have to reconcile their view of themselves as good parents with the fact that their child has been taken away because they have been deemed to be an inadequate parent.

The birth parents of children adopted from care have very high levels of problems that lead to and indicate social exclusion. Neil's survey (2000) of 104 children adopted from care found high rates of personal and psychological difficulties amongst the birth parents. Almost half (45%) of birth mothers had a mental health problem; a third (34%) had a learning disability; over a quarter (28%) had a drug or alcohol problem; and a quarter (23%) had a criminal record. Indices of social disadvantage were also extremely high. Sixty-eight per cent of birth mothers had never been employed and less than five per cent owned their own house. In 13 per cent of cases, one or both birth parents were of minority ethnicity, an over-representation compared to the general population. Issues of personal, psychological and social disadvantage and exclusion were central to the reasons why the children were removed from their family and placed for adoption. Pre-existing difficulties such as mental health issues or substance misuse may be exacerbated by the loss of the child, and at the

same time the birth parents' ability to cope with the loss may be compromised by their preceding difficulties (Neil, 2003; After Adoption,
2007).

There is very little significant research that explores the feelings of
birth relatives whose children are adopted from care. During the 1990s,
the Department of Health funded a series of adoption research projects
(summarised in Parker, 1999) but none of these studies included interviews with birth relatives. However, some small sample research has been
carried out. As with relinquishing parents and those whose children are in
long-term care, similar themes emerge from reports of the work of the
Parents without Children support group for birth parents in contested
adoptions (Mason and Selman, 1997; Charlton et al, 1998). The impact of
losing a child in this way is described as being devastating and long-
lasting. Feelings of isolation and emptiness were common, as were ongoing worries and thoughts about the child and his or her welfare and a
negative impact on health including sleep difficulties, weight loss, poor
appetite and vivid dreams. All parents interviewed said that they were
desperate for information about their child's welfare and that they would
have liked more information about the adoptive placement. Birth relatives
also experience a lack of sympathy and support from the community; they
are viewed as bad parents who are responsible for their own misfortunes.
Having a child adopted from care carries huge social stigma and has been
described as the last social taboo (Charlton et al, 1998).

The first wave of the Contact after Adoption study included interviews
with 19 birth relatives, all of whom remained in face-to-face contact with
their child or grandchild (Neil, 2003). This study found that it was
possible for birth relatives to reach a point of accepting and even feeling
positive about the child's adoption, even if the adoption had initially been
strongly resisted. Face-to-face contact with the adopted child was seen by
most birth relatives as helping them to accept the adoption both because
it reassured them of the child's welfare and because it reinforced the
position of the adoptive parents as the child's psychological parents.

The second wave of the same study (approximately seven years post-
placement) included interviews with 62 birth relatives, the majority of
whom had their child adopted through compulsory proceedings. Birth

relatives involved in indirect (letter) contact were included in this wave of the study, as were those birth relatives who took part in wave one (those who were having direct contact). A qualitative analysis of data explored the different ways these birth relatives accepted or did not accept the child's placement for adoption, and three patterns were identified (Neil, 2007a). The first pattern, "positive acceptance", was where birth relatives were able to accept that the adoptive parents were both legal and psychological parents of the child. They expressed positive views about the adoptive parents and positive feelings about the outcomes of adoption for the child, and often expressed that, although they had not wanted the adoption, things had worked out for the best. The second pattern, "resignation", was where birth relatives again accepted the reality that adoptive parents had taken over the legal and psychological role. They did not, however, view this as a positive resolution; narratives about how and why the adoption occurred were marked by feelings of passivity, powerlessness and a sense of being unable to control events. These birth relatives expressed strong feelings of worthlessness, depression and unresolved grief. The final pattern, "anger and resistance", was used to describe birth relatives who continued to resist the concept of the adoptive parents as the child's psychological parents. Negative feelings about the adoption were turned outwards towards other people and high levels of anger and blame of others were expressed.

Positive acceptance was associated with being a grandparent (as opposed to a parent) and with having face-to-face contact (as opposed to letter contact). The attitudes of birth relatives were seen to both influence contact arrangements (what contact was allowed and how contact progressed) and to be influenced by them in turn. Whether birth relatives did or did not positively accept the adoption was, unsurprisingly, linked to the establishment of collaborative working relationships with adoptive parents (Neil, 2009). The study suggested that some of the negative consequences of adoption for birth relatives can be alleviated if good quality post-adoption contact with adoptive parents and the child can be established.

The process of adoption

The process and consequences of having a child adopted from care need to be seen as further compounding social disadvantage and exclusion. The legal process of adoption is protracted and the emotional impact for the birth parent starts when the child is initially removed, if not before. The experience of a child going into care may precipitate a crisis. An After Adoption report into services in Wales (2007, p13) described parents' lives 'spiralling out of control'. Freeman and Hunt (1998) studied the perspectives of parents in care proceedings. They found that services offered to families before they reached court were sometimes inadequate; few parents felt they had participated in decision making; most felt ill prepared for court proceedings – instead, they felt marginalised, intimidated and confused; the majority of solicitors did not have specific expertise in this area of law; and, little support was available following proceedings.

Ryburn (1994) reported on interviews with members of 12 families who lost a child in contested adoption proceedings. Feelings of having been treated with a lack of respect by social services were commonly reported and such treatment was described by families as destroying the possibility of them working co-operatively with departments. Contested adoption proceedings may create or reinforce parents' feelings of betrayal, worthlessness and failure, as uncompromising evidence about their lack of abilities and maltreatment of their children is presented, sometimes by a social worker they may have understood to be "helping" them (Ryburn, 1994). Charlton et al (1998) reported birth parents' perceptions that information used in court was irrelevant or not checked out. Parents felt that social workers concentrated on the children and lost interest in them once the plan for adoption had been decided. Furthermore, these parents were often concerned that other children might be removed. Jackson (2000) found that birth mothers had concerns that the child might receive inaccurate information concerning the birth family. They felt that there was no opportunity for their strengths and positive feelings towards their children to be acknowledged.

The role of support for birth relatives

The need for birth relative support services is apparent from research on the psychological impact of adoption and on the experience resulting from a child's removal in contested legal proceedings. The psychological impact on birth parents of having a child adopted has been conceptualised in terms of "additional psychological tasks" (additional in this context meaning that parents keeping and raising their birth child do not have to deal with such issues). Triseliotis *et al* (1997) summarised these for birth relatives as being able to come to terms with feelings such as loss, guilt and self-blame and to recognise and accept emotionally that, although they remain the biological parents of the child, they will not be his or her psychological parent. Accepting the reality of roles and relationships after adoption may be impeded not only by feelings of loss, but also because their new role as a "birth" parent is undefined. Birth relatives' ability to address these psychological tasks, and to accept support to do so, will be compromised by the extent of their preceding problems, and by their experience of the adoption process itself.

There is growing research evidence that the adjustment of relinquishing birth mothers can be promoted if the mother retains some contact with her child after adoption (Iwaneck, 1987; Etter, 1993; Christian *et al*, 1997; Cushman *et al*, 1997). Support services for birth parents are important, not only for the welfare of the parent, but also for the well-being of their children, since it is now usual for some form of contact to be included in the adoption plan (Parker, 1999; Neil, 2002a). The ability of birth relatives and adoptive parents to work collaboratively over contact is a major factor in determining whether or not contact is likely to benefit the child (Triseliotis, 1980; Festinger, 1986; Grotevant *et al*, 1999; Lowe *et al*, 1999; Neil *et al*, 2003; Smith and Logan, 2004; Neil, 2009). However, many studies have also found that over time many birth mothers do not keep up planned contact, largely because without support it is very hard to manage the painful feelings that such contact can arouse (e.g. Etter, 1993; Berry *et al*, 1998; Logan, 1999; Young and Neil, 2004). Research suggests that it can also be hard for parents of children in care to maintain contact with their children over time (Aldgate, 1980; Millham *et al*, 1986; Masson *et al*, 1997). It may be that provision of support services can help birth relatives to keep up a level of contact which is supportive to the child (Neil, 2003) and prevent unresolved emotions hindering the parents' ability to work with agencies (Ryburn, 1994). The linking of contact support services and birth relative support services may prove beneficial (Neil, 2007b).

Birth relatives' experiences of support services

While research is scarce on birth relatives' experiences of adoption support services, there is some relevant research on service users' experience of social work services more generally (Mayer and Timms, 1970; Howe, 1993; Cree and Davis, 2006; Doel and Best, 2008). This research demonstrates that service users value the quality of the relationships with their social worker. They value workers who are honest, direct, trustworthy, respectful and friendly. They want workers who will listen, accept them and be non-judgemental. They want them to be knowledgeable and to be able to provide practical as well as emotional support. They value services which are flexible, responsive, reliable and accessible and available for as long as they are needed.

There is little research on the provision of adoption support services for birth relatives. Greater availability of support and opportunities to talk about the adoption of their child have been found to be related to better adjustment in some research studies on relinquishing birth mothers (Winkler and van Keppel, 1984; Howe et al, 1992). Winkler and Van Keppel (1984) found that better adjustment was related to opportunities to talk through feelings about the adoption, especially in the first year that followed. In addition, women who received support regarding the adoption from their friends or family fared better in the long run. Similarly, Bouchier et al (1991) found that mothers were more likely to cite their relinquishment experience as their most stressful life event if they had not received support in the following 12 months. Those who were given support, whether from family, friends or professionals, had better emotional health scores than those who did not. The importance of support in mitigating the loss is suggested by these findings.

Systematic research into services offered to support non-consenting birth relatives is lacking, although some descriptions of services have been published. Because of unresolved feelings of anger and betrayal, birth relatives may find it hard to use any support offered by the agency involved in removing their child. Such feelings may impede parents' willingness to, and/or comfort with, working with agencies over post-adoption support or contact arrangements. There may be additional barriers in accessing services for relatives of minority ethnicity. Charlton *et al* (1998) noted that feelings of shame and guilt may be exacerbated for parents judged by workers of a different ethnic background to themselves. Harris (2005) pointed out that one in five children for whom adoption is the plan are of black or minority ethnicity. She held focus groups of black birth relatives to ascertain their experiences of birth relative support. Participants identified a number of barriers to access, including lack of information and racist attitudes of staff. Harris suggests that concentrating on birth mothers and birth parents reflects an ethnocentric view of the family. Suggestions for improving access for relatives of minority ethnicity included making services available to members of the extended family, locating drop-in services in the community, having black workers with relevant linguistic skills and putting information leaflets in mosques, libraries, and community centres.

Types of support service

Services to help birth relatives of adopted children could take a number of forms, and could be provided before or after adoption, by the placing agency or an independent agency. Triseliotis *et al* (1997) outlined a comprehensive list of services that could be provided to help birth relatives. This includes providing information about adoption; advice on obtaining legal representation; involvement in planning the child's future, including selecting adoptive parents; preparation for meeting with the adopters; help with exploring their wishes about contact; provision of written non-identifying information about the adopters; support with mourning the loss and recognising the ongoing nature of this need; and information about future sources of help, including the Adoption Contact Register.

Before Adoption, a subgroup of After Adoption in Manchester, initiated a pilot project to help parents in contested adoption proceedings (Charlton *et al*, 1998). The parents in this project reported their greatest need to be advocacy, alongside counselling. Advocacy, in this case, meant having someone to explain "what is going on", to accompany parents to important meetings and to help them put their point across to professionals. Providing information and helping parents role-play in preparation for important meetings were other important aspects of pre-adoption birth relative support (Charlton *et al*, 1998). Although such empowerment did help some birth parents to take a more active role in decisions about their child's future, in some cases the project workers found that the provision of such services made social workers feel anxious about parents becoming more challenging.

Charlton *et al* (1998) also described the importance of individual counselling for birth parents: an opportunity to talk things through with another person, to be heard and understood but not judged. Hughes (1997), herself a birth mother, gave a firsthand account of what counselling can achieve. She describes how having another person to hold and contain her pain until she could manage it herself was vital in her process of coming to terms with her experience: 'This I see as being the most valuable and meaningful thing which M. did for me: that a counsellor can do for a birth mother. It involved a willingness to accept the pain we experience without escaping into the notion that this can somehow be made better' (p 9).

A further model of support for birth relatives is group support. Again, there is no published research that has systematically evaluated the efficacy of such support, but practice descriptions are available (Perl and McSkimming, 1997; Harris and Whyte, 1999; Jackson, 2000; Post-Adoption Centre, 2000). A major advantage of groups reported across these publications is that they can help diminish people's sense of isolation, and hence increase self-esteem. In the words of one birth mother, 'What a relief it was sharing our experiences which were so alike. It was like a cleansing of the soul . . . We had all suffered what we saw as a form of punishment as we all thought at the time we were basically bad people' (Harris and Whyte, 1999, p 44).

Services to birth relatives could include contact support services. As has been outlined above, not knowing what has happened to their child is a major source of anxiety for birth parents, an anxiety that can complicate grief resolution. Yet although birth relatives may want contact after adoption, practical and emotional barriers often stand in the way of the maintenance of good quality contact. Some birth relatives who remain in contact with their adopted child, through either meetings or letters, may receive services to support them in maintaining contact. Although such services may not be aimed at promoting birth relative adjustment, they may nevertheless serve this purpose if good quality contact is the outcome. Some birth relatives in Neil's study of Contact after Adoption reported receiving services to help them maintain face-to-face contact, and these were generally viewed as helpful (Neil, 2002a, 2002b), especially when birth relatives had many problems of their own. However, few birth relatives having indirect contact said that they had received any help or support to write letters (Young and Neil, 2004). Supporting birth relatives to be a resource to their adopted child can be undertaken within specialist birth family support services, and such work may also include helping parents to be involved in life story work, or writing a letter for the child to read when they are older (e.g. Mason and Selman, 1997; Charlton *et al*, 1998).

Finally, birth relatives may use general support services not specifically related to adoption, for instance, health services or counselling. This is especially likely to be true for the birth parents of children adopted from care, who generally have a multiplicity of social, physical and psychological difficulties. It may be that through some of these services, birth relatives can obtain help for adoption-related problems. For example, Sass and Henderson (2002) studied 66 birth parents in the USA and found that 42 per cent had received therapy at least once. Therapists who enquired about or addressed adoption issues were perceived as being significantly more helpful than those who had not.

Support services since the 2002 Act

A Commission for Social Care Inspection (CSCI) report found that more than half of all agencies inspected between 2003–2006 met or exceeded the national minimum standards pertaining to birth relative support, and all voluntary adoption agencies did so by the third year (CSCI, 2006, p 19). Agencies were judged to be good at providing or commissioning independent support services for birth parents, assisting with contact planning and ensuring that adopters understood the importance of contact. However, agencies were less successful at monitoring the quality of birth parent support services and ensuring the engagement of birth parents, particularly birth fathers. In terms of access to services, the report concluded that support 'usually works best when it is independent and there is a choice about when and how it can be accessed' (CSCI, 2006, p 4).

A report focusing on independent support services for birth parents and relatives in Wales and issues affecting engagement with these services was commissioned by the Welsh Assembly and prepared by After Adoption (After Adoption, 2007). Key issues affecting access included the complex ongoing needs of the parents and that professionals who made referrals did not understand the variety and scope of the services offered by the independent agency. There was a tendency to presume that "counselling" was the predominant service, which could mean that referrals were not received in a timely manner or that the referral did not reflect the parents' needs.

Problems with engagement and take-up of services have been highlighted in reviews of their services commissioned by After Adoption. A review of the birth relative service in Merseyside (After Adoption, 2008) looked at referrals received over a three-year period (2001–2004). In that time, the helpline received 161 referrals in total, 65 per cent from social services, 23 per cent self-referrals and 12 per cent from other sources such as probation, a solicitor and a learning disability support worker. The timing of referrals from social services appeared to be related to significant events such as the final hearing in care proceedings, a farewell contact or an imminent adoption order. Of those birth parents who were referred, 50 per cent did not respond when contacted or decided not to take up an appointment and this applied equally to those who had self-referred. A further 10 per cent attended only one appointment. Another After Adoption report focused on adoption support for young birth mothers with addiction difficulties in Teesside. The report makes recommendations for improving take-up of adoption support services, including: making adoption workers accessible in frontline services;

stressing the need for persistence in efforts to engage birth relatives through repeated offers of support; and by partnership working to increase other services' understanding of the impact of adoption on their clients (Camelot Foundation and After Adoption, 2008).

Summary

This chapter has outlined the legal and policy framework relevant to the research. Relevant literature exploring the experiences of birth relatives, and of the role of support services in helping birth relatives, has been reviewed. Key points are as follows:

- The current legal and policy framework stresses the lifelong impact of adoption on birth relatives and advises that birth relatives should be 'treated fairly, openly and with respect throughout the adoption process' (Department of Health, 2001, p 23).
- The Adoption and Children Act 2002 requires local authorities to ensure that parents have access to an independent support worker once adoption is identified as the plan for their child.
- Birth relatives who lose a child to adoption may experience long-term problematic feelings of loss, depression, guilt, shame, anger, and anxiety about the adopted child. Social support to help deal with these problems is often lacking.
- Birth relatives whose children are adopted in contested proceedings are often particularly vulnerable, with multiple pre-existing problems. The experience of the legal process as disempowering makes it difficult for them to trust professionals and take up subsequent offers of support services.
- Small-scale studies suggest that various types of service including advocacy, group work and counselling support may be helpful to birth relatives in negotiating the adoption process and adjusting to their child's adoption.
- Information about, or post-adoption contact with, the adopted child can also help some birth relatives deal with the impact of adoption.

2 Summary of findings from the mapping study

This chapter gives an account of the first stage of the research project – the survey which mapped services supporting the birth relatives of adopted children and services for contact across England and Wales. The survey's aims were to identify and describe the range and type of birth relative and contact support services provided by local authorities (LAs), voluntary adoption agencies (VAAs) and adoption support agencies (ASAs) in those countries. Although this mapping study looked at two areas of post-adoption support (support for birth relatives, and support for post-adoption contact), this chapter mainly focuses on reporting findings that relate to supporting birth relatives.

Methodology of the mapping survey

Three data collection methods were used: questionnaires, telephone interviews and focus groups. Questionnaires were sent to all local authority adoption agencies, VAAs and ASAs in England and Wales. The agencies included were all of those registered with the Commission for Social Care Inspection (CSCI) in England and the Care Standards Inspectorate (CSI) for Wales on 21 July 2005. Data were gathered in the second half of 2005. Questionnaires were sent to Adoption Support Services Advisers (ASSAs), managers with designated responsibility for post-adoption support in all LAs, and to the directors of VAAs and ASAs. Two hundred and fourteen questionnaires were sent out, and 135 completed questionnaires were returned – an overall response rate of 63 per cent. Of these, 98 were from LAs, 28 from VAAs and nine from ASAs.

The questionnaire contained 23 items which were a mixture of open and closed questions. The questionnaire was divided into three parts: Part 1: the role of the ASSA (or equivalent person in VAAs and ASAs) within the agency; Part 2: the arrangements the agency had in place to support the birth relatives of adopted children; and Part 3: the service provision in relation to supporting post-adoption contact. This chapter draws mainly on data from Part 2 – the questions about birth relative support services. This section of the questionnaire included nine questions.

1) How does your agency plan to provide independent support services to birth relatives?
2) How can birth relatives access services?
3) What is your experience of getting birth relatives to use these services?
4) What types of services have you provided or commissioned in the last 12 months?
5) If you use other agencies to provide services, what type of financial arrangements do you have with these agencies?
6) How do you help (or plan to help) birth relatives of minority ethnicity?
7) How do you help (or plan to help) birth relatives who have additional challenges related to physical/learning disabilities, mental health or addiction?
8) Do you evaluate your services, and if so, how?
9) Do you include the participation of birth relatives in service planning, provision or review, and if so, how?

All of these questions, with the exception of Question 4, were open questions with a blank space for respondents to write in. Question 4 was answered by completing a table with "yes"/"no" answers, allowing agencies to say whether or not they had provided various different types of support services.

In Part 3 of the questionnaire, very similar questions to those above were asked about how agencies were providing post-adoption contact support. In addition, this section of the questionnaire also contained a case vignette – an outline of a face-to-face contact arrangement between an adopted girl, her adoptive parents, and the birth mother. Problems in the contact were described and agencies were asked to provide a description of how their agency might respond to a request from the adoptive parents to help manage this complex contact situation. Respondents' qualitative responses were analysed using a thematic analysis, the focus of which was the underlying attitudes of workers in this field of practice (see Neil, 2007b for full details).

The agency questionnaires were examined and 60 agencies were selected for follow-up telephone interviews with ASSAs or other dedicated adoption support staff. Each interview was guided by a semi-structured schedule, tailored individually from each returned questionnaire, so that the researchers could probe, develop and clarify areas of particular interest. Ten of these had a particular focus on issues of economic costings and contractual arrangements in the purchase and provision of services. Two focus groups were held (one on birth relative support services and the other on contact support services) with adoption staff. These included those from a range of agencies across sectors, of varying sizes and in different parts of England and Wales, including inner-city and other urban areas with significant black and minority ethnic populations. These provided further opportunities for information gathering and for group participants to share and exchange views on the range and effectiveness of service provision and delivery.

Findings of the mapping survey: support services for birth relatives

This chapter summarises the key findings relevant to the area of birth relative support services. Full details of this survey can be found in the final report (Sellick *et al*, 2006) and in an overview of key findings (Sellick, 2007).

How support for birth relatives was being provided

Although every local authority provided or commissioned some form of birth relative support service, the availability and type of support services varied widely across England and Wales. Questionnaire respondents were asked to complete a matrix indicating whether they had provided the following 10 types of services to birth relatives over the previous 12 months: assessment; information and advice; support groups; therapy; counselling; intra-/inter-agency liaison; assistance with direct contact; assistance with indirect contact; casework; and advocacy. Focusing solely on the number of types of services provided to birth relatives, it was found that 25 LAs (26%) provided all 10 types of service specified in the questionnaire. Fifty-nine LAs (60%) provided between seven and nine of

31

the services, 10 LAs (10%) provided between four and six of the services, and four LAs (4%) provided less than four of the 10 services. Support for direct or indirect contact was most likely to be available (95% said they provided this, although this included provision for children and adoptive parents as well as birth relatives); and the provision of advocacy (62%) and therapy for birth relatives (58%) were the least likely to have been provided. It was clear, therefore, that the location of birth relatives broadly determines what might be on offer.

In terms of how LAs were discharging their responsibilities to provide support services to birth relatives, four patterns were identified indicating differences in the extent to which these services were provided in-house, or in partnership with external agencies. There were very few ($n = 11$, 11%) LAs which did not use the independent sector at all to provide support for birth relatives. Over two-thirds of agencies ($n = 67$, 68%) indicated that they relied on one or more external agencies to provide support to birth relatives on their behalf. A further 15 per cent ($n = 15$) said they sometimes used the independent sector to supplement in-house support, for example, via the spot purchase of services from an agency or independent worker. Five agencies provided their birth relatives with support via a local authority consortium arrangement.

Thirty-seven VAAs and ASAs completed open questions relating to the provision of birth relative support services. In three cases the responses given by the VAA were not clear enough to code. Fifteen of the other 34 agencies were involved in providing independent birth relative support services on behalf of LAs and 18 were not.

Sixteen VAAs were *not* involved in providing independent support services on behalf of LAs. However, all of these agencies described some level of involvement with birth relatives. The three main types of services provided were: counselling or support to birth relatives previously known to the agency whose children had been adopted via the agency; intermediary services to birth relatives seeking contact with their adopted child; and assisting contemporary birth relatives whose children were placed via their agency, with post-adoption contact (usually an agency mediated letter exchange between the adoptive parents and birth relatives). Two of these 16 agencies specified that they did occasionally provide independent birth relative support on behalf of an LA, but on a "spot purchase" basis. There were nine VAAs which said they were involved in providing independent support services on behalf of LAs. One of these provided services for two LAs and all the others worked with just one LA.

Turning now to the adoption support agencies: one ASA had no involvement in supporting birth relatives as it was an adoptive parent-led support organisation; two ASAs (both former VAAs which no longer placed children) only provided intermediary or other support services to "their" birth relatives; the remaining six ASAs all had extensive involvement in supporting birth families. One of these agencies was user-led and provided a variety of support services to birth relatives on the basis of their membership of that organisation or via "spot purchase" arrangements with LAs. The other "big five" ASAs all had multiple partnerships with LAs, one agency having as many as 32 service level agreements. Two of these five ASAs provided support services only to birth relatives from their partnership LAs. The other three ASAs said they had additional funding from grants or trusts that enabled them to help birth relatives who were not funded by partnership LAs, for example, through telephone helplines, drop-in centres, or specialist schemes in prison settings.

The issue of low take-up of services

We asked the following question in the questionnaire: 'We know from initial investigations that it can be quite hard to get birth relatives to use these services. What is your experience? How do you promote your services?' About half of the respondents (58 agencies) replied in such a way that we could code whether they agreed or disagreed that service take-up was a problem, and difficulties with take-up were identified by the vast majority of these ($n = 52$, 90%). For example, one London borough said that contemporary birth relatives 'rarely keep appointments made to discuss matters in depth and do not attend counselling sessions with our independent counsellor'. Another LA, which contracted with an independent agency, said, 'Take-up of the service offered by the outside voluntary agency has been very low, especially for parents in current contested cases'. In some cases, respondents indicated that they had problems getting birth relatives to begin using services, but that once they did so they usually continued and found it beneficial. Others said they had experienced problems with birth relatives beginning and sustaining involvement. Six agencies (10%) indicated that they did not have a problem with service take-up.

Suggestions from practitioners who took part in the interviews and focus groups helped us to understand why service take-up was a problem. Three main factors were identified. Firstly, many birth relatives express anger towards the local authority responsible for removing their child and placing them for adoption and do not trust that any service can be truly independent or even appropriate to their needs. Secondly, there are a number of additional difficulties affecting the lives of many birth relatives (such as mental illness, learning difficulties, substance misuse and addiction and unstable lifestyles) which make them a hard-to-reach group of potential service users. Thirdly, many respondents commented on the difficulties they experienced in reliably receiving referrals from child and family social workers. As one said, 'Where agencies leave it down to the child's social worker and rely on their commitment to refer, difficulties arise particularly because of their caseload priorities, lack of adoption work experience and the high staff turnover in many local authority departments'. This issue of referring birth relatives for support and the implications of differing referral routes for uptake of services are explored in further detail below.

Routes to services
The different ways that birth relatives could gain access to support services varied considerably. Referral routes were categorised into seven different models, which varied in respect of whether the referral would be dependent on individuals or automatically generated by the system at a particular point in the adoption process (Cossar and Neil, 2009). The models also varied according to whether they offered one or multiple routes to access the service.

Model 1: On request. These agencies provided services to birth relatives as and when parents approached them and requested this.

Model 2: Individual information and self-referral. In this group, eligible birth relatives were informed of the availability of services, and given contact details of the service provider.

Model 3: Social worker referral and on request. Birth relatives in this group could access services via social worker referral. Although agencies may have provided services on request from birth relatives, they did not provide individual relatives with information and the means to self-refer.

Model 4: Information, self-referral and social worker referral. Here, birth relatives were given information about services and could self-refer. In addition, social workers could also refer people for support.

Model 5: Information, self-referral, social worker referral and other professional referral. This group is as above (Model 4), except that, in addition, the agency provided information about their services to other professionals in contact with birth relatives, and they would accept referrals from these others, such as GPs, solicitors, CAFCASS officers and guardians, family centre workers, adult care workers (e.g. mental health, learning disabilities, drug/alcohol), domestic violence units, and Citizens Advice Bureau staff.

Model 6: Automatic allocation of independent in-house worker. These were agencies which told us that when adoption was planned, birth relatives were automatically contacted by, allocated to or offered a link worker from the adoption service who was not the worker for the child.

Model 7: Automatic referral to support service. These were agencies which told us that they automatically referred all eligible birth relatives to a specialist support service (this could be in-house, but most were provided by independent agencies). This referral could be triggered at a number of stages in the adoption process.

There are potential advantages and disadvantages to the various models (see Cossar and Neil, 2009, for a detailed discussion). Birth relative-dependent models (1 and 2) required the relative to self-refer. This might be viewed as empowering, in that birth relatives could theoretically choose whether or not to get in touch with a service and the right time for them to do so. However, arguably such models place too much responsibility on a vulnerable group who may have complex needs predating the adoption, who may have been alienated by the contested adoption process, and who may be distrustful of professionals. Birth relatives who have not played a central part in the adoption process may not be informed of services at all and this may apply in particular to non-resident fathers, siblings and extended family members.

In the social worker dependent models (Models 3 and 4), the main responsibility for making the referral rests with the child's social worker. The child's social worker is in a good position to make a timely referral for birth relative support, given their ongoing knowledge of the adoption plan and close involvement with the family. However, there are also potential pitfalls to this route as it is dependent on the quality of the relationship between the childcare social worker and the family, and on the worker's knowledge and inclination as to when or whether to make the referral.

Multiple referral routes include self-referral, social worker and other professionals (Model 5). Including other professionals may increase the likelihood of a timely referral from a professional whom the birth relative trusts. However, the use of other professionals to refer relies on these professionals being informed about adoption support services and increases the onus on such services to provide training and up-to-date information to numerous professionals.

Some agencies employed a system of automatic referral (Models 6 and 7). This sometimes involved automatic allocation of an in-house worker or automatic referral to an independent service. Referrals could be triggered by the system at different points in the adoption process. Timing of the referral could have an impact on uptake of service. Having an "opt out" rather than an "opt in" system could raise issues of confidentiality if the birth relative was not aware that their details were being passed to another agency. Using an in-house worker may be advantageous in establishing good working relationships with child care social workers. However, it is questionable as to what extent they would be viewed by birth relatives as independent.

Specialist services

Few specialist services for birth relatives of black or minority ethnicity had been developed at the time of the mapping survey and these were generally centred on interpretation and translation. Likewise, few agencies reported that they had developed services to take account of the mental health or learning disability needs of some birth relatives.

Commissioning and the role of the independent sector

As outlined above, the majority of LAs had arrangements with VAAs or ASAs to supplement their own provision of birth relative support services. However, the low take-up of services had led to some LAs withdrawing these commissioning arrangements in order to provide services in-house. Staff from independent providers expressed concern about the uncertainty and instability this was causing them, as well as the risk that birth relatives would question the independence of services provided by the LAs and use these even less.

Linking birth relative support to contact support

Adoption staff from many agencies suggested that birth relatives were more willing to take up support services if these were connected to the contact they were having with their adopted child. Examples included assisting birth relatives in writing contact letters, reminding those who used letterbox contact of the availability of support services and getting workers supervising direct contact to explain support services to birth relatives.

Services supporting contact: findings relevant to birth relative support

Most adopted children will have a plan for indirect or direct post-adoption contact with one or more birth relatives. The Adoption Support Services Regulations 2003 (DfES, England) and 2004, 2005 (National Assembly for Wales) give adoptive parents, adopted children and birth relatives the right to request an assessment of need regarding contact arrangements, and require agencies to maintain services to assist contact arrangements.

This section summarises key findings about contact support that are relevant to birth relative support.

The key role of local authorities in managing post-adoption contact arrangements

Our survey found that the vast majority of local authorities were supporting post-adoption contact in-house, as opposed to using the independent sector. The bulk of their activity related to supporting letterbox contact: on average, agencies were supporting 15 letterbox arrangements for every one face-to-face arrangement. In many agencies, sophisticated and thorough systems for the provision of indirect letterbox contact had been developed. The same was not true of support for face-to-face contact, which agencies seemed to mainly deliver as a response to expressed need. The finding that local authorities largely tend to retain responsibility for supporting post-adoption contact is relevant to birth relatives because it indicates that in most cases the birth relative and the local authority will continue to need to have some level of working relationship once the adoption order has been made.

The needs of birth relatives for support with post-adoption contact: workers' attitudes

In examining workers' responses to the complex contact case vignette, the differences between how people said they would respond to the child and adoptive parents as opposed to the birth mother, in both LAs and VAAs, were marked in many cases. A willingness to provide a support service directly to the child was widespread and often accompanied by remarks about the need for the child to be the focus when thinking about contact. Compared to supporting the child and adoptive parents, supporting the birth mother was mentioned less often. The types of support that workers suggested they might offer included emotional support and referral to other services. However, the most common response to the birth mother was when discussing the boundaries around contact and the impact on the child – often with the threat that contact might be terminated. Less than one-third of respondents suggested referring the birth mother (who was described as being depressed and having problems coping with the contact situation) for additional help, for example, from mental health workers, the GP, or independent birth relative support providers. Very few respondents suggested an intervention that was focused on working jointly with the birth mother and the adoptive parents to establish a collaborative working relationship. We argued that this could suggest that many workers see the needs of birth relatives and adoptive parents as competing as opposed to potentially overlapping (Neil, 2007b). Indeed, in some cases the birth mother was seen primarily in terms of what harm she might pose to her child, rather than in terms of what she could contribute. Whilst many of the agencies responding to the case vignette clearly did see this complex contact situation as an opportunity to help the birth mother, this was not true of all.

Summary

This chapter has discussed the findings from our mapping study which explored the provision of birth relative support services and contact support services within local authorities, voluntary adoption agencies, and adoption support agencies in England and Wales. Key findings are as follows.

• Although all LAs were providing or commissioning support services for birth relatives, large variations in the range and type of services available in different areas were apparent.
• The independent sector (ASAs and VAAs) have a very active involvement in providing independent support services to birth relatives – only 11 per cent of LAs did not work with any independent agencies in providing services.
• The low take-up of support services by birth relatives was identified by many agencies, this being attributed to the complex problems of birth relatives, the antagonism and mistrust many birth relatives feel towards professionals, and to problems in achieving effective referrals from children's social workers to adoption teams and independent agencies.
• Different models of how birth relatives could access support services were identified. These varied in the extent to which birth relatives

themselves had to take the initiative to acquire a service, and the extent to which social workers in local authorities were responsible for making referrals.

- Contact support services were mainly provided in-house by LAs, necessitating an ongoing relationship between birth relatives and these agencies.
- An examination of social workers' attitudes towards supporting contact suggested that the needs of birth relatives for support in maintaining contact after adoption may not always be recognised.
- Links between contact support and birth relative support were identified: it is likely to be helpful for birth relative support services to include help with post-adoption contact and for contact support services to include provision for supporting birth relatives.

3 The "Helping birth families" study: design and methods

This chapter describes our research questions, the design of the study and our methodology. More complicated aspects of our methodology are described in greater detail within the relevant findings chapters.

Research questions

The "Helping birth families" study aimed to address the following research questions:

1. **How many birth relatives are referred for support services and how many take up these services?**
   - Does this take-up of service differ between agencies, or by gender, ethnicity and type of birth relative?

2. **What are birth relatives' experiences of adoption and how are people affected by the experience?**
   - What are birth relatives' views about why adoption was planned for their child or grandchild?
   - What is the process of adoption like for birth relatives?
   - How did birth relatives feel when their child was going to be adopted and how do they feel about this now?
   - What levels of psychological stress do birth relatives experience? (Does this differ by gender or birth relative type? Does psychological distress diminish over time?)
   - How do birth relatives cope with the loss of a child to adoption? (Are there differences between birth mothers, birth fathers and grandparents? Does coping change over time?)

3. **What types of support services do birth relatives report using and what are their experiences of these?**
   - How many birth relatives reported using a support service?

- What types of activities/services do birth relatives report support agencies as providing?
- How many different types of support were included in each person's service?
- Are there differences between birth mothers, fathers and grandparents in self-reported service use?
- What aspects of support services do birth relatives value or not value?
- How satisfied overall were birth relatives with the support services they received?
- What are the reasons why some people do not use support services?
- What other sources of support do birth relatives identify?

4. **How much do support services cost?**
- How much of a support worker's time does it take to support a birth relative and what are the different costs of providing each support service?
- How many and what types of different services did support agencies provide to each person in the study over a one-year period?
- What does it cost to support birth relatives for a one-year period? Does this cost differ by agency?

5. **What is the impact of support services on birth relatives?**
- What impact does receiving a support service have on birth relatives' psychological distress?
- What impact does receiving a support service have on birth relatives' coping with adoption?
- Does satisfaction with services vary by service amount and type?
- Does the cost of services relate to outcomes and if so how?

Summary of the study design

This study was conducted in collaboration with eight participating agencies: one voluntary adoption agency; three local authorities; and four adoption support agencies. The aims of the project were both to understand birth relatives' subjective experiences and to measure service use and outcomes looking at the relationship between these. Therefore, a mixed methodology employing both qualitative and quantitative methods was employed. The study had a longitudinal design, following up birth relatives over a 15-month (mean) period and measuring the "intervention" they received over this time gap.

The research involved three strands:

- **The intensive study**: Collecting interview data and a mental health questionnaire measure from birth relatives at two points in time, approximately 15 months apart. Reference groups of birth relatives (involving 14 birth relatives – 11 birth mothers, two birth fathers and one birth grandmother) – were consulted at the planning, analysis and results stages of this part of the study.
- **The service take-up survey**: Survey of referral and take-up information from participating agencies.
- **The economic analysis**: Collection of data from birth relative support workers detailing the resources that go into providing services, and also the collection of data about service use over a 12-month period by individuals participating in the intensive study.

The intensive study

Ethical approval and research governance
Prior to beginning the study, approval for the research was obtained from the Association of Directors of Social Services (in 2005). The study was also approved by the UEA's School of Social Work and Psychology ethics committee. Individual agencies then needed to give their own approval, and in most cases a member of the research team visited the agency to discuss this. One local authority (LA 3) had a formal research governance procedure that had to be completed before participation could be agreed.

The agencies
The eight agencies participating, and the number of birth relatives recruited via each, are detailed in Table 3.1 below. From our mapping survey, we had already learned a great deal about which agencies were providing birth relative support services and we had made a number of contacts with people in the field. We had a number of aims in mind when

recruiting agencies. We wanted to recruit people from a range of agencies rather than just one agency, so that we could study people's experiences of receiving support from a wide variety of sources; we wanted some larger agencies which could help us recruit significant numbers of people; we wanted to include all three agency types (adoption support agencies, local authorities and voluntary adoption organisations); and we wanted to ensure that we could recruit some birth relatives of minority ethnicity.

Table 3.1
Participating agencies and numbers of birth relatives recruited via each agency

		N	*%*
ASA 1	Provides birth relative support services for five LAs	23	31.5
ASA 2	Works with 13 different LAs to provide birth relative support services	20	27.4
ASA 3	A small ASA contracted by one LA to provide birth relative counselling services	4	5.5
ASA 4	A large ASA with several regional branches across England and Wales; contracted by many LAs to provide birth relative support services	14	19.2
VAA 1	Commissioned by one LA to provide independent birth relative support services	5	6.8
LA 1	A Welsh Unitary LA; provides birth relatives with "in-house" services but also refers to an ASA if required	1	1.4
LA 2	Ethnically diverse London borough; provides some birth relative support in-house, and can refer people to an ASA	1	1.4
LA 3	Ethnically diverse London borough; provides some birth relative support in-house, plus can refer people to an ASA	2	2.7
	Recruited via personal contact	3	4.1
Total		**73**	**100.0**

Table 3.1 shows that the vast majority of people in the sample were recruited via agencies in the independent sector, just over 78 per cent being drawn from three ASAs. As each of these three ASAs was working with a number of LAs, the birth relatives in our study will have had their children adopted via a wide range of LAs. Only four birth relatives came from the three participating LAs. We are not entirely clear why so few birth relatives responded from LAs. It may have been that people were less receptive to requests passed on via the agency that had removed their children or that birth relative support services were less well developed in these agencies and fewer people were using them. Alternatively, this could have resulted because the birth relatives within these authorities – especially the two London boroughs – may have been harder to reach/engage in the research because of the more transient and ethnically diverse populations living in these areas. The study can thus say little about how birth relative support works in agencies where this is provided mainly or exclusively in-house.

Recruiting birth relatives

An extensive process of consultation with our birth relative consultant groups was undertaken prior to attempting to recruit birth relatives into the study. The aims of this consultation exercise were to help us understand what might motivate birth relatives to take part, and how to prepare the recruitment materials appropriately. Key points of advice that we received were: to make recruitment materials look professional and attractive; to keep the wording brief and clear; to emphasise that taking part in the study was a chance to help other birth relatives in the future; to include a freephone number via which people could contact us; and finally, to try and resist agency attempts to screen out some birth relatives from being invited – the point being that birth relatives should be allowed to make up their own minds rather than to have the agency decide on their behalf. We followed all of this advice and had leaflets professionally designed and accompanying websites set up. Invitation packs included leaflets and reply slips and postage-paid envelopes. Potential participants could contact us by the reply slip, by the freephone number or via email, the first two options being used more frequently than the third.

We had to negotiate with each agency individually about how to invite birth relatives into the study. Our aim was to try and recruit birth relatives at, or shortly after, the time they were referred to, or began to use, services. Our criteria for the inclusion of people in the study were as follows:

a) They were adult birth relatives from families where a decision had been made for a child to be adopted.
b) The adoption decision had been made in the last year or, in the case of VAAs and ASAs, the birth relative's involvement with or referral to the agency had begun in the last year.
c) The adopted child was under 18 years of age at the time of interview. We told agencies that we did not want them to pass on invitations to birth relatives to whom they were providing intermediary services.

Our mapping study had revealed that service uptake was an issue, and we wanted to explore the reasons why this might be so. Hence, we wanted to include in the study people who were eligible to use services but had not, as well as those who were using services. We asked agencies to pass on the invitation pack to birth relatives who had been referred in the previous six months, and also to those referred into the service over the following six-month period. Most agencies were reluctant to just post the invitation to people who met the criteria, arguing that they preferred to pass on invitations by hand when meeting with service users or posting them to existing service users, perhaps after a preliminary telephone contact. In fact, only one agency (ASA 1) agreed to send out the invitation pack to all people who had been referred; all other agencies dealt with the issuing of invitations in a variety of ways, but mainly through targeting existing service users rather than the much broader pool of referred people. The reasons agencies gave for wanting to undertake the recruitment in this way was that they felt strongly that this would achieve a good response rate. We did discuss with all agencies the feedback we had from our service user consultation groups – especially the encouragement to let birth relatives decide about participation themselves, as opposed to not inviting people in order to "protect" them. It was not possible for us to keep track of how many packs agencies gave or sent out, and so we cannot report the response rate.

Birth relatives who responded were contacted by telephone or letter, the study was explained further and questions were answered. If the birth relative felt happy to proceed, a date was arranged for the interview to take place. People were given the option of either a telephone or face-to-face interview. The target sample of at least 70 birth relatives were recruited with relative ease within the planned timescale. The helpful advice we received from our birth relative consultant groups seemed very useful in enabling us to achieve this.

Semi-structured interviews

Two interviews were conducted with each birth relative (on average) 15 months apart (range 12–21 months) in order to provide a longitudinal aspect to the study. The interview schedule was devised in consultation with the assistance of our birth relative consultants groups. A fairly open style of interview was felt to be most appropriate by both the research team and the birth relative consultants. The key reason for this was the sensitivity of the topic and the need therefore to allow the interviewee to proceed at their own pace and explain things in their own words. Consequently, the few closed questions with fixed responses that we had planned to ask were not used. The interview at Time 1 covered the following areas:

- basic details about self;
- the adopted child – how they came to be adopted;
- the child's placement/ progress – any meeting with adoptive parents – views of adoptive parents;
- contact arrangements with the adopted child;
- support for adoption – from birth relative support services and other sources and views of these;
- current feelings about the child and about the adoption.

In addition, birth relatives of minority ethnicity were asked if they had particular needs related to their ethnicity and, if so, how they had been supported with these.

The interview at Time 2 did not ask relatives to repeat historical information about the background to their child's adoption. With regards to the other areas of the interview, birth relatives were asked to provide an update on what had happened since the last interview and how they were feeling now.

Consent was obtained verbally from birth relatives at the beginning of the interview and was recorded. On the advice of our birth relative consultants, written consent forms were not used as the majority of interviews were by telephone, and because we expected many birth relatives to have literacy problems. Birth relatives were asked to give permission for the interview to be recorded; they were informed about the confidentiality policy and were told about their right to withdraw, take a break or skip certain questions. People were informed about the intended goals of the study. Interviews were recorded either digitally or on tape. Birth relatives who were using support services were asked to give their permission for us to ask the appropriate agency to fill in the "service use diary" (see this chapter, below). All interviews were fully transcribed. Birth relatives were offered either a small cash gift (if we interviewed them in person) or a store voucher in thanks for their participation.

The Brief Symptom Inventory (BSI)

The BSI (Derogatis, 1993) is a 53 item self-report symptom inventory that measures psychological symptoms. It has the advantages of other self-report measures: it provides subjective information about internal states that may not be accessible to an observer, it is economical to administer, does not require high levels of professional training, and is easy to score and interpret. It is one of a matched series of tests and rating scales in the Psychopathology Rating Scale series, which includes the longer 90 item Symptom Check List (SCL-90-R). Derogatis (1993) reports that the convergent validity of the BSI with both the Symptom Check List and the MMPI (Minnesota Multiphasic Personality Inventory) is impressive. The BSI can also be used to identify which individuals are "case positive" (suggesting a clinically significant level of psychiatric symptoms) in terms of their psychological distress.

The BSI test was administered at the end of the interview with birth relatives. If the interview was face-to-face, the interviewee was given the choice of completing the measure themselves (after receiving instructions) or answering out loud – (we offered this option because a high percentage of our sample was likely to have some literacy problems). If the interview was by telephone, in most cases the interviewee completed the measure over the phone with the interviewer. In a few cases, the measure was sent and posted back later. The test was administered at Time 1 and Time 2.

Data analysis in the intensive study

The analysis of data in the intensive study took four main forms. Firstly, some interview data were analysed purely qualitatively, using thematic analysis (e.g. birth relatives' experiences of the adoption process). Secondly, other interview data were used to produce categories based on researcher ratings (e.g. "satisfaction with service use"). Thirdly, we developed a coding methodology to measure "coping with adoption", producing numerical ratings that could be treated as interval data and analysed quantitatively. Fourthly, the BSI measure was scored according to the manual. Some analysis was conducted solely on Time 1 data. Some analyses used both interviews together to produce "overall" ratings, and some analyses were repeated using Time 1 and Time 2 data. The key ways in which the data were analysed are summarised in Table 3.2 on the next page, and the methods by which analyses were undertaken are outlined below. The chapters reporting results contain further details of our analyses.

The analysis of interview data progressed through various stages, as detailed below.

Stage 1: Broad content coding

After transcription, data were entered into the qualitative data analysis software, Nvivo 2. We then coded this data into "nodes" around different topics/areas of interest. These were based around the topics we had asked about in the interview and our initial ideas about important themes within the data (both from our experience gained doing the interviews and from previous research). These nodes enabled us to gather together all the relevant information around certain themes. For example, one node was called "dual connection", and here we coded anything the birth relative said that indicated their acceptance or otherwise of the adoptive parents and of the child's membership of the adoptive family, and their general feelings or comments about the child being a member of two families.

49

Table 3.2
An outline of data analysis in the intensive study

Time 1 data	*Time 2 data*

Experiences of adoption:

- Problems in parenting
- The immediate crisis
- Going through care and adoption proceedings
- After placement – contact issues

Service use (coding looks at services used overall, i.e. using both interviews, or just the first interview if the person did not take part at Time 2)

- Emotional support
- Support with contact
- Advice and information
- Advocacy and liaison
- Peer support
- Number of types of services used

Experiences of service use: (coding looks at experiences of services used overall, i.e. using both interviews, or the first if the person did not take part at Time 2)

- Features of support services that were valued by birth relatives
- Reasons why some people did not use services
- Descriptions of what other support was used by birth relatives
- "Satisfaction with service use" researcher ratings

Outcomes: (coding repeated on both waves of data)	Outcomes: (coding repeated on both waves of data)
- Accepting dual connection	- Accepting dual connection
- Feelings about the outcomes of adoption for the child	- Feelings about the outcomes of adoption for the child
- Dealing with the impact of contact on self	- Dealing with the impact of contact on self
- "Coping with adoption" scale	- "Coping with adoption" scale
- Brief Symptom Inventory scores	- Brief Symptom Inventory scores

Other nodes were large and gathered both descriptive and evaluative content. For example, the node "adoption support" was used to gather together all the data about what birth relative support services the person had received and what they thought about these. The final number of nodes we used at Time 1 was 15. As this coding was completed by a number of members of the team, written protocols were prepared and used.

Stage 2: Case summaries
In order to keep a sense of birth relatives as individuals, and to understand the context of individual parts of their interview, case summaries were written for each person, initially using the Time 1 interview. The case summaries were also an essential tool for team working, enabling people who had not conducted the interview or worked on the Nvivo coding to understand the issues in each particular case. They also enabled us to collate key demographic information, for example, age, ethnicity, details about the adopted child, etc, as we had no other sources of data about these. With the Time 2 interview data, we updated the summary to record any key changes in the case, and to summarise the data we were using to make overall researcher ratings and ratings that were repeated at both time points (see Table 3.2 above). A template including written guidelines on writing summaries was prepared and used. Although the case summaries took time to construct, we did find that they were an invaluable tool in the subsequent data analyses.

Stage 3: Thematic analysis
Where our aim was primarily to describe birth relatives' experiences (e.g. experiences of having their child adopted), our approach was to conduct a thematic analysis. Our methodology was an adapted version of that described by Boyatzis (1998) and drew on existing theory as well as being data-driven. The processes undertaken in Stages 1 and 2 significantly facilitated this process as we had already identified any key issues and themes and, in some cases, categories. Both the case summaries and the relevant Nvivo nodes were then used to systematically identify and illustrate themes, and to write the relevant sections of the report.

Stage 4: "Quantifying" qualitative data

For some of our research questions, we needed to quantify qualitative data, e.g. to look at birth relatives' satisfaction with adoption support, and here we developed protocols for researchers' ratings. The most complex quantification of qualitative data was in our construction of the "coping with adoption" scale, and the details of how we undertook this are given in Chapter 11. All quantitative data were entered into SPSS and appropriate statistical analyses (as described in the findings chapters) were carried out.

The service take-up survey

The aim was to gain an overall picture of the volume of birth relative support activity within our participating agencies, to look at take-up of services and to be able to compare the birth relatives in our study with the population of those using services. Participating agencies were asked to fill in a "brief referral information" sheet for every new person referred to their service over a six-month forward period. The (non-identifying) information this data sheet asked for included:

- date of referral
- who referred the person
- gender
- age
- relationship to adopted child
- reason for referral
- ethnicity

We then contacted agencies 12 months after the end of this six-month data collection period and we asked them to fill in the second half of the sheet. Here they indicated whether the person had or had not used any services, along with very brief details of what they had provided to the person. The eight participating agencies all took part in this survey. The number of birth relatives about whom data was returned was 495.

The economic analysis

The economic analysis aimed to estimate the cost of providing support services to birth relatives over a 12-month period. In order to do this, it was first necessary to estimate the number and type of services that each birth relative was provided with and, importantly, to cost this provision by estimating the time that support workers spent providing each service. To undertake each task, two data collection tools were developed: case worker diaries and service use diaries.

Case worker diaries

Time diaries, referred to as case worker diaries, were developed in order to accurately estimate the amount of time spent on each of the various services and activities (counselling and therapeutic support; contact support; general and practical support; other support) provided by case workers to birth relatives. Each of the eight agencies in the study was asked to invite these case workers to complete the diaries over a four-week period (or two fortnightly periods).

The case worker diaries were designed to provide details of both direct activities (those specifically involving the service user in face-to-face or telephone contact) and indirect activities (including working indirectly with, or on behalf of, the service user, e.g. writing letters, making telephone calls, travelling and administrative activities). These indirect activities are often overlooked, but without this preparation time it can be impossible to effectively provide the face-to-face services. Caseworkers were asked to indicate the time they had spent in relation to the following activities (the definitions below are taken from the case worker diary):

Counselling and therapeutic support
This is delivering or arranging therapeutic/counselling support to clients. It includes listening and talking to the client where the focus of your work is their emotional wellbeing as it relates to the experience of and adjustment to their child's adoption.

53

Contact support
This includes helping clients to write letters, taking them to contact meetings or talking to them after contact meetings.

General and practical support
This includes getting information and advice, attending meetings/case reviews with the client, advocacy, etc.

Other support – client-focused
This is other support with/for client. Help may be given with other areas of the client's life that is not specifically related to the child's adoption, e.g. financial, housing, addiction or mental health problems.

Other work – not client-focused
This is other work related to birth relative support that is not client-focused, for example, training agency workers in birth relative support.

Analysis of case worker diaries

The case worker diaries were aggregated for each respondent to provide an estimate of the total time commitment for each case worker providing support services and also the total number of cases supported. The time commitment was divided by the number of cases to provide an estimate of each worker's average time commitment for each support service and activity combination. These were then aggregated and further summarised to provide a representation of the average time commitment across the whole sample. The total average time commitment for each support service was then valued (see below). Additional analysis considered the direct and (total) indirect activities (that is, the sum of indirect client work, travel and administration) and compared them to provide some estimate of hidden time costs.

Valuation of time

The value of the time committed to providing each support service was estimated by applying published unit costs. The Personal Social Services Research Unit (PSSRU) estimated that, in 2007, one hour of client-related work for a social worker who earns an average salary of £26,748 costs £39 per hour (Curtis, 2007). Therefore, if it takes an average of 90 minutes to provide one session of counselling to a birth relative, this is estimated to cost £58.50 (39 x 1.5). The published unit costs we used were represent-ative of the social work system in 2007. These unit costs were estimated from much earlier work that attempted to cost child care provision (Knapp et al, 1984). The methodology of estimating unit costs is complex (see Beecham, 2000), and new research has recently come to light which suggests that the previous estimate of overheads (e.g. running costs, personnel and management costs, building costs: that is, the costs that cannot be attributed to any one individual case) was an underestimate (Selwyn et al, 2009). Therefore, the costs presented in this study are likely to also underestimate the true cost of providing birth relative support services.

Service use diaries

In order to cost the provision of support, it was necessary to record the support provided (or not provided) to service users in the study. To undertake this task, a "service use" diary was developed. This diary was to be completed for each birth relative recruited to the study for a 12-month period. The service user's case worker logged which and how many of the services the service user was provided with in each month of the year. Services included in the diary were: needs assessment; information and advice; support groups; therapy; counselling; assistance with face-to-face contact; assistance with letterbox contact; casework; advocacy; other services. It was suggested to agencies that this diary should be kept inside the case file, and completed each time the case file was accessed.

Analysis of service use diaries

The information collected in these diaries was aggregated for each type of support service and the total number of services provided to each service user was also calculated. This allowed for the estimation and description of the level of support for the "average" birth relative in the study.

Total cost estimation and analysis

The unit costs of support services (as estimated using the case worker diaries) were combined with the use of support services (as collected in the service use diaries) and the total cost of providing post-adoption support services to birth relatives was calculated. The three specific case worker activities (as described in the time diaries) were mapped to the nine specific support services (as listed in the service user diaries) to estimate the total cost of service provision for any one individual in the study.

The total cost of the "average" birth relative was estimated, and analysis was undertaken to compare costs across agencies, specifically the three ASAs which provided the lion's share of the sample.

In addition, the analysis also examined the relationship between total resource use and total cost, and a range of measures as follows:

- self-reported use of services
- satisfaction with service use
- BSI "case positive"
- the BSI global severity index
- the "coping with adoption" scale

Summary

This chapter has outlined the five key research questions, the design of the study, and the methodology used to answer the research questions. Key points are as follows.

- This study aimed to cost and evaluate services provided to the birth relatives of adopted children. The five key research questions we endeavoured to answer were:
  - How many birth relatives are referred for support services and how many take up the services?
  - What are birth relatives' experiences of adoption and how are people affected by the experience?
  - What types of support do birth relatives report using and what are their experiences of these?

- How much do support services cost?
- What is the impact of support services on birth relatives?
- In order to answer these research questions, we worked with eight different support providers: three local authorities, one voluntary adoption agency and four adoption support agencies. Most birth relatives were recruited via the independent birth relative support providers (ASAs and VAAs).
- The intensive study, which collected data from 73 birth relatives and which had a longitudinal design, followed birth relatives over a 15-month time gap, interviewing people at the beginning and end of this period. The key outcomes focused on were: satisfaction with support services (measured by researcher ratings from the interviews); coping with adoption (measured by a scale developed by the research team); and psychological well-being (measured by a standardised questionnaire – the Brief Symptom Inventory).
- In the service take-up survey, we collected information about 495 birth relatives referred to our participating agencies over a six-month period.
- The economic analysis involved the collection of data from case workers to cost different support activities and data from agencies about the services used by birth relatives in the study over a 12-month period. We calculated individual costs for individual service users and related these to the outcomes measured in the intensive study. We also related outcomes to people's self-report of service provision.

4 The referral and service take-up survey

This chapter provides more information about the agencies participating in our study in terms of their volume of referrals of birth relatives for support services and the numbers who take up the services on offer. The data that agencies provided us with about their referrals over a six-month period enabled us to look at factors that may relate to the take-up of services and also to compare our sample of birth relatives with the wider population of birth relatives referred to services. The point in time when agencies began the six-month period of collecting data about referrals varied from agency to agency, but was generally late 2005/early 2006. We asked agencies to keep a record (on specially designed "brief referral information" sheets) of all referrals to the service over the six-month period, recording the following information, if it was available, on the top half of the form:

- relationship to the adopted child;
- referral source;
- ethnicity;
- the agency that had placed the child for adoption (or was planning to do so);
- the point in the adoption process at which the referral was made;
- reason for referral.

The numbers of cases for which agencies gave information about the point in the adoption process when the referral was made, or the reason for referral, was less than half the sample, and so no further analysis of these factors was carried out. We asked agencies to assign a non-identifying case identifier to each referral, to enable them to identify the person one year later. We also asked agencies to enter the follow-up date on the bottom of the form – this being 12 months from the date of referral. Then, 18 months after the start of the data collection period, we contacted agencies again and asked them to fill in the second half of the data collection sheet for each referral. Here the agencies were asked to specify whether or not the person had used any services ("yes" or "no") and to give brief details of which services they had used and if and why the service provision had ended.

The volume of referrals for birth relative support

Table 4.1 shows how many referrals each service provider received in the six-month data collection period. In most cases, agencies assured us that they believed these records to be accurate. However, in the case of the large organisation with several branches (ASA4), not every branch returned the data sheets, hence these figures do not represent the total volume of work for this agency. The agencies dealing with the largest volume of referrals were the same three agencies from which we gained most of our interview sample (ASAs 1, 2 and 4). However, the proportion of cases from each agency in the interview sample are not the same as in this referral survey sample. In particular, ASA 4, the national organ-isation, clearly had the most referrals but this agency did not provide the largest proportion of cases in the interview sample. This may suggest that, in the case of such a large organisation, there are many more people to communicate with about the purpose and expectations of the research, perhaps meaning that our messages about who to invite into the study were not always transmitted. The other agencies all had one central office and one key person with whom we were liaising about the research. The other interesting point to note in this table is the very low volume of referrals to two of the three in-house birth relative support services (the two London local authorities); this may in part explain why we were unable to recruit many people via local authorities. We therefore cannot say that experience in these local authorities can be generalised to apply to other local authorities using in-house provision.

The right-hand column in Table 4.1 also shows, for each agency, the number of local authorities which were pursuing the adoptions of the children. This information was available in almost all cases ($n = 478$, 97%). These data indicate that the three local authorities only took referrals of their "own" birth relatives. With the independent agencies, in

59

most cases the placing agencies were the local authorities with which independent providers had contractual arrangements. In some cases, however, VAAs/ASAs took on other clients, such as people who live within their area but whose children may have been adopted in another area, or where provision was spot purchased from local authorities. Hence the number of placing agencies referring to the agency in some cases was greater than the number of agencies with which they had contractual arrangements.

Table 4.1
Numbers of referrals in the participating agencies over the six-month data collection period

	N	% of 495	Number of placing LAs
ASA 1	94	19	6
ASA 2	71	14.3	16
ASA 3	15	3	2
ASA 4*	269	54.3	39
VAA 1	23	4.6	2
LA 1	14	2.8	1
LA 2	8	1.6	1
LA 3	1	0.2	1
Total	**495**	**99.8**	**68**

*Not all branches of this organisation took part in this survey.

Across the sample of 495 referred birth relatives, 66 placing local authorities were identified (NB. the figures in the right-hand column of Table 4.1 total 68 because two local authorities referred birth relatives to more than one independent agency).

Take-up of services and sources of referrals

In only a few cases were agencies able to supply further details about what services people had used or how long they used them for – in most instances, they just answered the "yes"/"no" question about whether services were used. Across the eight agencies, 56.3 per cent of people referred for support services had used at least one session of support in the 12 months following their referral. This take-up rate refers to birth relatives who were *referred* for support. This group is likely to be only a subset of birth relatives who were *eligible to be referred* (that is, all the birth relatives of children for whom adoption was planned). This research has not measured the numbers of birth relatives eligible for services, but figures from the study do give some indications that by no means all eligible birth relatives were being referred. For example, local authorities which had contractual arrangements with our participating agencies seemed to vary very widely in terms of how many referrals they made to the independent agency. The largest number of referrals made by a local authority to one of the participating agencies was 42. However, in several cases, the independent agency participating in the study received as few as one referral of a birth relative originating from one of their "partnership" local authorities. We cannot say whether or not these local authorities had other arrangements in place to meet the needs of birth relatives in their area. However, these low figures do concur with findings from the mapping study that low volumes of referrals from local authorities can be a significant problem.

In our interview sample, 65.8% of birth relatives had used support services; a chi-square test showed that there were no significant differences between the two samples in terms of whether or not birth relatives used services ($\chi^2 = 2.31$, $n = 549$, $df = 1$, $p = .128$ ns). Table 4.2 shows the take-up of services within the eight participating agencies.

As this table shows, the percentage take-up rate across the eight agencies differs dramatically. In the case of the two London boroughs (LA 2 and LA 3), these had low numbers of referrals (in one case, LA 3, only one referral) but most people were using services. This suggests perhaps that social workers only refer birth relatives to the adoption team if it seems likely that the person wants a service. The other agency, LA 1, referred more people to their in-house service, but only about one-quarter used services.

The take-up rate of referred birth relatives in the independent support providers varied from 19.1 per cent in ASA 1 to over 70 per cent in

Table 4.2
Take-up of services across agencies

	N of referrals	N of people who took up service	% of agency referrals*
ASA 1	94	18	19.1
ASA 2	71	27	43.5
ASA 3	15	5	33.3
ASA 4	269	191	73.7
VAA 1	23	16	69.6
LA 1	14	4	28.6
LA 2	8	6	75
LA 3	1	1	100
	495	268	

*These figures exclude 19 cases where agencies did not provide follow-up data.

ASA 4. These figures may reflect the relative success of different agencies in engaging with those who are referred. For example, ASA 4 was a well established organisation with several years' experience in providing services to birth relatives. However, from our discussion with agencies and information gleaned in our mapping study, we would argue that differences in take-up rates may also be due, at least in part, to the different methods by which people are referred to independent agencies.

Agencies were asked to indicate on the brief referral data sheets who had referred each individual to the service. This part of the form was only completed in 360 (72.7%) of cases and Table 4.3 shows the results. The two biggest referral sources were social services or the social worker (just over half of referrals came from the latter) and the birth relative themselves (just over one-third of people self-referred). Although many agencies told us they would accept referrals from a range of sources, less than 10 per cent of people were referred by other professionals (e.g. their solicitor or doctor), friends or other sources.

Table 4.3
Referral routes into services

Referral source	N	%
Self-referral	134	37.2
Social services/social worker	195	54.2
Other professional	24	6.7
Friend or family	1	0.3
Other	6	1.7
Total	**360**	**100.1**

In the three local authorities, all referrals were made in-house. We looked at whether routes into services differed across the five different independent agencies, and for this analysis we combined the three smallest categories into one (other professionals, friends and family, and other). Table 4.4 shows the different referral routes across four of the five independent agencies. Unfortunately, ASA 1 did not complete this part of the form, but subsequent discussion with the agency indicated that although referrals were accepted from birth relatives themselves and from other professionals, the vast majority of their referrals came directly from their partner LAs.

Table 4.4
Referral routes in four independent service providers

	Self-referral		Social services		Other	
	N	%	N	%	N	%
ASA 2	15	28.3	34	64.2	4	7.6
ASA 3	5	33.3	8	53.3	2	13.3
ASA 4	108	41.4	131	50.2	22	8.4
VAA 1	4	17.4	18	78.3	1	4.3

The data in Table 4.4 show that there were differences between agencies in terms of who refers birth relatives. ASA 4 had the most self-referrals and the least social services referrals, and this may, at least in part, explain their high service take-up rates. The fact that ASA 1 said the vast majority of their referrals came from social services may explain their lower take-up rates. To examine whether referral routes were associated with service take-up, a chi-square test was carried out comparing those who were referred by social services (n = 178) with those who self-referred or were referred by others (n = 163). Of those who referred themselves or were referred by people other than social services, 79.8 per cent took up services. In contrast, of those who were referred by social services, 56.7 per cent used services. The association between referral route and service uptake was highly significant ($\chi^2 = 20.62$, $df = 1$, $p<.001$). However, these differences in who refers birth relatives cannot explain all the variations. For example, VAA 1 has the opposite pattern to ASA 4 – in most cases, their referrals are from their one partner LA, and yet they also achieved nearly 70 per cent take-up rate. This may reflect the intensive efforts this agency had made in developing a positive awareness of the service within the partner agency.

When considering the take-up rates of different agencies, it is important to bear in mind not just who refers birth relatives, but the extent to which all eligible birth relatives are referred. For example, the agency with the lowest take-up rate, ASA 1, had an arrangement with a large local authority to automatically refer birth parents after the adoption panel had agreed the plan for adoption. So, theoretically, this agency was referring 100 per cent of eligible birth relatives, but only a minority were taking up the service. Other independent agencies described different methods of referral, for example, some placing agencies may only refer birth relatives who express interest in an independent service or who do not want to use in-house provision; or they may just inform birth relatives that independent services are available, but leave them to self-refer if they wish to use them. In these cases, only a small percentage of eligible birth relatives are likely to be made known to independent providers, but these people have been preselected on the basis of their willingness to receive a service. So the differences in take-up rates between agencies need to be considered with reference to how – and especially how many – of the eligible pool of birth relatives are referred to the service.

The ethnicity of birth relatives referred for services

The ethnicity of the referred birth relative was known in 71.5 per cent of cases ($n = 354$). It was not the case that ethnicity was missing mainly for birth relatives who had not used services: of those 136 people whose ethnicity was not given by the agency, 42 per cent had used services. Of those whose ethnicity was recorded, 91.5 per cent of people were described as "white British". Of those who were not white British, three (0.9%) were "other white", and the rest were from nine different ethnic groups, the largest of these (five people, 1.4%) being African-Caribbean. Interestingly, take-up of services was somewhat higher amongst birth relatives from minority ethnic groups (22 of 28 used services, 79%) compared with white British people (122 of 189 used services, 65%), but this association was not statistically significant ($\chi^2 = 3.46$, $df = 1$, $p = .06$). There were no significant differences between the interview sample and the referral sample in terms of the ethnicity of birth relatives ($\chi^2 = 1.95$, $n = 427$, $df = 1$, $p = .16$).

The relationship of referred birth relatives to the adopted child

The relationship of the referred birth relative to the child was known in almost all cases ($n = 476$, 96.2%). Two-thirds of those referred for support services were birth mothers ($n = 319$, 67%). Less than one in five of those referred were birth fathers ($n = 93$, 19.5%). Four referrals were of birth parent couples. Of the remaining 60 other birth relatives (12.6%), 20 were grandparents, 31 were siblings, and nine were other relatives. In our interview sample we had 60 per cent birth mothers, 26 per cent birth fathers and 14 per cent grandparents; a chi-square test showed that there were no significant differences between the two samples in terms of the proportion of mothers, fathers and other relatives who took part ($\chi^2 = 1.79$, $n = 545$, $df = 2$, $p = .41$). However, in the interview sample the "other" relatives were all grandparents: we did not interview siblings or extended family members such as aunts and uncles. The take-up of support services by different types of birth relative is detailed in Table 4.5. In this table, grandparents, siblings and other relatives are all included in one group of "other" birth relatives (the four birth parents couples are excluded from the analysis).

Table 4.5
Take-up of services by birth relative type

Birth relative type	N in survey sample*	N who used services	% of birth relative type who used services
Mother	303	179	59.1
Father	91	41	45.1
Other relative	60	37	61.7

* Excludes 25 cases where data about service use was missing.

The data in Table 4.5 show that while about 60 per cent of birth mothers and other relatives took up services, only 45 per cent of birth fathers did so. A chi-square test showed that the association between birth relative type and use of services was statistically significant ($\chi^2 = 6.32$, $df = 2$, $p<.05$). So not only were far fewer birth fathers referred than birth mothers, those who were referred were less likely to take up offers of support.

Summary

This chapter has explored the referral of birth relatives to the eight participating support service providers, and looked at the issue of take-up of services. Key findings are as follows:

- Over half (56%) of birth relatives referred for support used services over a one-year period, but this differed dramatically by agency. These differences could be explained both by differences in the success of agencies in engaging people who were referred, but also by the referral routes into services.
- Birth relatives who referred themselves or were referred by others (not social services) were significantly more likely to take up services than those referred by social services.
- Two-thirds of birth relatives referred for support services were birth mothers. Less than one in five of referred birth relatives were birth

fathers. Siblings, grandparents and other relatives made up 13% of those referred. Birth fathers were significantly less likely than birth mothers or other relatives to have taken up services.

- Birth relatives of minority ethnicity made up 8.5 per cent of those referred for support services. No significant association between ethnicity and service take-up was found.
- This referral survey enabled us to compare our interview sample to the broader pool of birth relatives referred to the participating agencies. No significant differences between the two samples in terms of ethnicity, birth relative type and whether or not people used services were found.
- This survey sample of referred birth relatives may not be represent-ative of birth relatives of adopted children as a whole, many of whom may not be referred for specialist adoption support services. The sample is likely to over-represent people who showed an interest in receiving support services.

5 The interview sample: birth relatives' characteristics and the background to the adoptions

This first part of this chapter describes the demographic characteristics of the birth relatives who took part in the intensive study, including some information about the adopted children. The second part then draws on birth relatives' accounts of why their child or grandchild was taken into care and had become the subject of an adoption plan. We did not collect data from adoption agencies about the reasons for adoption, and so what is reported here is very much the birth relatives' own perspective on the adoption. We recognise that had we spoken to local authorities, their accounts of the reasons why the children needed to be adopted may have been quite different. However, in order to understand the needs of birth relatives, it is necessary to understand adoption from their point of view.

The birth relative interview sample

Seventy-three birth relatives took part in the first round of interviews and over three quarters ($n = 57$, 78%) of people took part again at Time 2. Of those who dropped out, most ($n = 10$, 14%) could not be contacted (not at last address) or did not respond to letters or phone calls. Two people declined to take part and four people said that they would take part but did not keep scheduled appointments. Most people ($n = 46$, 63% at Time 1; $n = 40$, 70% at Time 2) were interviewed by telephone. The remaining interviews were carried out face to face ($n = 27$, 37% at Time 1; $n = 17$, 30% at Time 2); most of these were conducted in people's homes (at Time 1 three were held in prison and three at a venue such as the ASA, and at Time 2, one was held in prison).

The birth relatives in the study came from 61 different birth families. The sample included eight birth parent couples. Where both birth parents wanted to participate in the study, we encouraged people to be interviewed separately (indeed, this was a necessity for those being interviewed over the telephone). Four couples were interviewed separately, but four couples wanted to be interviewed face-to-face and together. Where we did interview people in this way, we tried to ensure that both parents gave individual answers to the questions. The sample also included parents and grandparents from the same birth families in four cases, and in each of these the birth parent was interviewed separately from the grandparent.

As Table 5.1 shows, over 85 per cent of our interviews were with birth parents, mostly birth mothers. Proportionally more birth mothers dropped out of the study (27.3% of mothers) compared to other groups of birth relatives (10.5% of fathers and 20% of grandparents dropped out).

Table 5.1
Relationship of birth relative to adopted child

	Time 1		Time 2	
	N	%	N	%
Birth mother	44	60.3	32	56.1
Birth father	19	26.0	17	29.8
Paternal grandmother	3	4.1	3	5.3
Maternal grandmother	6	8.2	4	7.0
Maternal grandfather	1	1.4	1	1.8
Total	**73**	**100.0**	**57**	**100.0**

The age of birth relatives at Time 1 ranged from 18–63 years old (mean = 35.2, sd = 11.3). Almost 90% of birth relatives were white (65 of 73, 89%). One person was South African Indian, two were African-Caribbean, and five were of mixed ethnicity. The proportion of interviewees from minority ethnic groups was the same at Time 1 as at Time 2.

At the time of the first interview, only 13 birth relatives were in full time ($n = 5$, 7%) or part-time ($n = 8$, 11%) employment. Thirty-one people described themselves as unemployed (42.5%), and over one-fifth ($n = 16$, 22%) said they were unable to work because of illness or disability. Seven people were looking after children or caring for relatives

(9.6%). Of the remainder, three people were in prison, two were students, and one was retired.

At the Time 1 interviews, 39 birth relatives (53%) were living with a spouse (n = 14, 19%) or partner (n = 25, 34%). Thirteen people described themselves as separated or divorced (19%), 19 said they were single (26%) and one was widowed.

The adopted children and grandchildren

Although most birth parents in the study had more than one child, the vast majority were not currently caring for any of their children. The birth parents in the study had between one and eight children (mean = 2.8, sd 1.6). One in five parents had only one child (n = 13, 20.6%). Seventeen people had two children (27%); 18 had three children (28.6%); and 15 had four or more children (23.8%). For just over 60 per cent of birth parents (n = 38, 60.3%), all of their children had been adopted or were to be adopted. Only four parents were looking after a birth child at the time of the first interview; in most cases the parents' other children were being cared for either by ex-partners, relatives or were in the care system. The ten grandparents in the study had between one and four children. The numbers of grandchildren each person had was not recorded. About two-thirds (n = 50, 68.5%) of the birth relatives in the study had actually had a residential caring role with their child or grandchild. Mothers were most likely to have been resident carers (n=35, 79.5% of mothers), whilst only 57.9% (n = 11) of fathers had been in this role. Four of the 10 grand-parents had, at some stage, been full-time carers for their grandchild.

Because many birth relatives had more than one child adopted (or to be adopted), with each person we identified an index child and the interview focused mainly on discussing this child. Since we wanted to focus on recent adoptions, in most cases the youngest child adopted (or to be adopted) was chosen as the index child. Forty-one of the index children were girls (56.2%) and 32 (43.8%) were boys. Eighty-five per cent of the index children were white (n = 62), one was African-Caribbean (1.4%) and the remainder (n = 10, 13.7%) were of mixed ethnicity.

Table 5.2 shows the age of the child at removal, the time since the child had been removed from the birth family, and the time that had elapsed since the adoption placement had been made (both of these latter figures are at Time 1). This reveals that in most cases we had interviewed people very close to the adoption or in the midst of the adoption process. In almost one-third of cases the adoption placement had not been made, and in some of these the plan was not yet finalised. In almost another third of cases, the child had been placed only within the last 12 months. Most of the children had been very young at the age of their final removal from the birth family, the majority being under the age of one and many of these having been removed at birth. The speed at which children were removed from home suggests the severity of concerns about their welfare.

Table 5.2
The age of the index children at removal, at interview and the time since their placement for adoption (at Time 1)

	Range (years)		*Mean*	*sd*
Age when left birth family care	0–4	Under 1 year: n = 47, 64.4% 1–2 years: n = 20, 27.4% 3 or older: n = 6, 8.2%	.67	1.07
Age at Time 1 interview	0–12	Under 2 years: n = 23, 31.5% 2–3 years: n = 31, 42.5% 4 or older: n = 19, 26%	2.95	2.53
Time since child placed for adoption	0–9 (*n* = 50)*	Not yet placed: n = 23, 31.5% <12 months: n = 22, 30.1% 12–23 months: n = 15, 20.6% 2 or more years: n = 13, 17.8%	1.3•	2.1*

* Based on only those who had been placed at Time 1.

Problems in parenting

Birth family problems leading up to the child's placement for adoption

Birth relatives were asked to talk about the reasons why their child or grandchild needed to be adopted. This section looks at what birth relatives said were the issues they felt affected the care of the child at the time he or she came into care. It includes issues reported to be affecting either birth parent. Birth relatives told their stories in their own words and their

71

narratives were coded in Nvivo under the "birth relative view of adoption" node. This node was analysed further to generate the following categories of problems.

- *Relationship difficulties*

This was restricted to difficulties between the birth parent and their partner and it included a broad range of problems such as domestic violence including rape, physical abuse and stalking. Others mentioned living in fear of their partner, anger problems or frequent arguments. Repeated separation and reunion, divorce and infidelity were also cited.

- *Mental health issues*

The most usual problem people cited was depression, including post-natal depression. Other problems included anxiety or stress, personality disorder and bipolar disorder. Some birth parents did not specify a "diagnosis" as such, but referred to being on medication or having other types of treatment, including having stays in psychiatric hospital. In several cases it was clear that parents' mental health issues were complex, longstanding and seemingly baffling to both the individual and to mental health professionals. For example, one birth mother said:

> *I had to go for a psychological assessment to see if I could have [my child] back and I failed on the mental health. They said I had mental health, but they didn't give me an illness for it. They gave me all sorts of labels and then came to one decision this year of Borderline Personality Disorder. Oh, but I had loads, I had stress disorder, I've had post-natal depression, I have had everything really, they said, and I have been on a lot of medication.*

- *Substance misuse*

This category included those who mentioned the use of alcohol or illegal substances as significant problems. In some cases the interviewee said that they themselves were drinking heavily or using drugs, for example, using crack cocaine whilst pregnant. In other cases the relative stated another person involved in parenting the child was misusing substances. For example, one birth mother commented about her partner, 'He had a severe drink problem, he had to be controlling it for twenty-eight days but he couldn't do it'.

• *Effects of own history/childhood*
Many relatives spoke about adversity within their own childhoods. This included experiencing numerous changes in carer as a child, being abused and growing up in care. Others had experienced traumatic events such as rape. One birth mother described her early childhood as follows:

I haven't had a very good upbringing, my mum basically when I was born didn't want to know. I was palmed off to quite a few different family members, my mum only kept me living with her for the extra money that she could spend on her cigarettes and that.

• *Problems with child*
Some relatives mentioned factors specific to the child that they felt made parenting more difficult. They referred to the child having particular health needs, to difficulties in bonding with a particular child and to competing needs between children. Several attributed some of their difficulties to the child's behaviour, for example, a birth mother commented:

It all started with Kaylee, she's my six-year-old, because she's got dyspraxia now . . . she was playing up, and I asked for help over the phone, and nobody did anything.

• *Birth relative health needs or disability*
This category included relatives who referred to physical or learning difficulties as a relevant factor. It also included some parents who referred to their own physical health problems as impacting on their ability to parent, and to one grandparent who commented on her age as a factor in the decision that she could not care for her grandchild long term.

• *Practical problems*
Some relatives described poor or inadequate housing as a factor. A birth father talked of work commitments which stopped him taking on the full-time care of his child, and others talked generally of financial difficulties.

73

- *Crime*

This category included relatives who were in prison at the time of the interview, or who were under investigation, or involved in criminal proceedings either as a witness or as a defendant. For example, one birth mother was convicted of manslaughter relating to a drugs overdose and imprisoned two weeks after her children were removed by social services.

- *Contact with sex offender*

A few relatives said that the family was in contact with a known or suspected sex offender or that the birth parent had been convicted or was suspected of a sexual offence against a child. For example, one father said that he could not be considered to care for his daughter because of a previous offence of indecent assault against a 14-year-old girl.

- *Problems with others (other than partner)*

This category included references to others causing difficulties such as an interfering ex-partner, violent members of the extended family or lack of support from extended family, and violence and abuse from people outside the family.

- *Bereavement or loss*

Bereavement or significant loss around the time that their child was removed was mentioned by some relatives, for example, one birth mother lost her sister and had a miscarriage in the months after her children were taken into care.

- *Immigration issues*

One birth mother mentioned that her partner was not allowed to take part in the residential assessment when he was found to be an illegal immigrant.

Table 5.3
Problems relatives cited as affecting the family at the time of the adoption

Issue	Number of cases in which issue cited	Percentage of cases in which issue cited
Relationship difficulties	30	41.1%
Mental health issues	24	32.9%
Substance misuse	23	31.5%
Effects of own history/ childhood	22	30.1%
Problems with child	18	24.7%
Birth relative health needs or disability	13	17.8%
Practical problems	12	16.4%
Crime	10	13.7%
Contact with sex offender	8	11%
Problems with others (other than partner)	5	6.8%
Bereavement or loss	5	6.8%
Immigration issues	1	1.4%

Table 5.3 shows the range of problems affecting the birth relatives and the frequency with which they were cited across the sample. The most commonly cited issues were relationship difficulties, mental health and substance misuse. Included in the table are all the factors the relatives acknowledged to be affecting them, although it is important to note that there might be disagreement with professionals about whether and to what degree the problems experienced were affecting the child and whether the plan for adoption was appropriate. It is quite possible that difficulties may have been present but not referred to in the interviews, so the data are very likely to underestimate the prevalence of these problems. For instance, mental health problems were cited by 32.9 per cent of the relatives. However, the standardised measure that we asked people to

complete (the BSI) suggested that the prevalence of mental health issues was likely to be much higher – on this measure, almost three-quarters of birth relatives were scoring within a clinical range (see Chapter 12). A background of poverty was suggested by the numbers of birth relatives who were unemployed (less than one in five of birth relatives in the study were in work). However, financial problems were cited by relatively few of those interviewed.

Many birth parents experienced multiple difficulties. Only a minority of birth relatives (8.7%) did not cite any problems which were affecting the family at the time their child was taken into care. Ninety-one per cent of birth relatives acknowledged some difficulty affecting the family. The most common number of problems cited by birth relatives was two with a mean value of 2.8. The range of problems referred to shows the diversity of the issues facing birth relatives. The co-existence and severity of the problems cited indicate the complexity of people's needs. The complex and long standing nature of problems experienced by birth parents is illustrated below.

Case study: Birth mother, Caroline

Caroline had a difficult teenage period, often in trouble with local gangs. She gave birth to her first child at 16, the result of rape by her mother's ex-husband. Her second child was born when she was 18. She struggled to look after the two children. Her partner did not help and they argued frequently. Caroline said that a neighbour phoned children's services, accusing her partner of being violent towards her; she denies this but said that he did wreck the house. Both children were removed from her care and placed with her mother. When it was realised that Caroline's mother's ex-husband was a risk, the children were placed in foster care. The birth parents were then offered a residential assessment. Things went badly wrong when Caroline discovered that her partner had started an affair with another woman at the assessment centre. Following this, she could not bear to stay there and abandoned the assessment. Children's services made the decision to work towards adoption.

Agreement with or opposition to the adoption plan

Birth relatives' agreement with the plan for adoption at the time that events took place was coded. It was felt that people's subjective feelings of agreement with the adoption plan were more important indicators than whether or not they legally consented to or contested the adoption. Some people referred to giving consent despite not wanting their child to be adopted or only when they could see no point in fighting against a decision that appeared to have already been made. There were cases where birth relatives chose not to contest the adoption after being told by their solicitor that they had no chance at all of getting the children back, or they simply lacked energy to fight what they considered to be a losing battle. At the same time, however, they still remained *internally* opposed to the decision. Others referred to not signing over consent even when they *did* feel it was best for their child to be adopted, as they did not want the child to feel in the future that they had been rejected.

As described above, most birth relatives acknowledged the existence of serious psychosocial problems impacting to some extent on parenting. Often some level of harm to the child was identified but the need for the child to have been adopted was often strongly disputed. A recurring theme through birth relatives' accounts was that of "unfairness". Further analysis revealed differences in agreement which varied according to the extent to which problems were acknowledged, the extent to which it was recognised that the problems were impacting on the child, and whether the birth relative felt that adoption was the best option for the child. Birth relatives' attitudes could be categorised into five groups, each of which is described below.

Group 1: Denies any problems

In this group, the birth relative claims there were no problems in their family and that the child was not (deliberately) harmed by them. Allegations of physical or sexual abuse are often flatly denied and anger towards and blame of professionals is often strongly expressed. In many cases, relatives refer to the fact that they have been victimised whilst other "worse" parents are allowed to keep their children.

Case study: Birth father, John

John's first child by a previous partner was adopted due to allegations of violence, which John disputes. John then married his current partner and they went on to have two sons, Michael and James. A nursery worker noticed that James had bruising and a black eye and contacted children's services. John says that James was bruised accidentally when he climbed up on the furniture and fell off. Medical opinion was that James had been punched, which John vehemently denies. During the assessment, children's services also reached the view that the children were being neglected and that the house was not habitable. John says that he did read the report but in the end he was confused as to why the children were adopted. He denies that he did anything wrong and feels that social workers were out to get him from the start. He blames the nursery workers, medical staff and children's services.

Group 2: Locates problems with other person/s

The birth relative admits problems in the birth family and concedes that the child was harmed or at risk of harm. But they emphasise that *they* were not the cause – it was someone else. In cases where birth parents were no longer together, one parent frequently identified the other parent as the person who was the danger to the child. In many birth parents' eyes, the fact that they had lost their child because of something somebody else had done (or failed to do) felt very unfair.

Case study: Birth mother, Jane

Jane had a difficult childhood, suffering prolonged sexual abuse. She married young and had a daughter who was sexually abused by an extended family member. Children's services were involved with this child due to her ongoing behavioural difficulties. Jane went on to another relationship and had two more children. She says that the younger children were taken into care because of their father, who was violent and controlling. She felt that she got mixed messages from social services. It was not clear to her whether she should leave her partner or try to patch things up. The assessment concluded that, in addition to the risk posed by her partner, Jane herself had mental health difficulties and was unable to be a good mother. Jane disagrees and feels that her own abuse and experience of being parented was held against her.

Group 3: Accepts problems in family, but disputes children's services' view of harm to child

This group comprises birth relatives who do identify problems in their lives. They either argue that the problems were resolved by the time adoption became the plan, or admit they have problems but deny that the problems impacted or were likely to impact on their child. Thus this group of birth relatives disagrees with children's services' view of current harm to the child.

Case study: Birth mother, Michelle

Michelle has three children. The youngest child – Peter – is the subject of the interview. He was taken into care aged two. Michelle has learning difficulties. Her partner moved in to help her after the baby was born. He was violent and Michelle was afraid of him. He moved out when she found out he was having an affair. The birth father and the grandmother phoned social services as they were concerned she could not look after the baby. Neighbours were also expressing concerns. Michelle was given advice about playing with the baby and told that she was struggling to meet his emotional needs. Michelle denies any problems with her parenting: 'It's not like I beat him . . . I smacked him but that's it – but my mum used to do it to me, I thought that's how you did it but I didn't bruise him . . . I didn't break any bones . . . there's not a lot of reasons to take Peter away.'

Group 4: Accepts concerns and supports adoption

In this group, the birth relative acknowledges problems in the birth family and concedes that these were likely to affect or had affected the child. They agree with the adoption plan. This group included two birth mothers who were primary carers for the child. It also included other grandparents and birth fathers (none of whom were resident carers for the child) who all felt that the birth mother could not care for the child and that they were not in a position to take over the care themselves.

Case study: Shirley, maternal grandmother

Shirley's daughter, Jo, had behavioural problems from the age of 14. She shoplifted and took overdoses. Children's services were involved when she became pregnant because the father was a drug user. After the baby was born, Jo was diagnosed with post-natal depression. The baby was taken into care and Jo was discharged from hospital. She went off the rails and ended up sleeping rough. Jo was eventually diagnosed with bi-polar disorder. Shirley initially wished to care for both her daughter and grandchild and planned for them to move in with her. However, she soon realised that she could not cope with the severity of her daughter's difficulties and care for her grandchild. She did not feel that her daughter could look after the baby adequately. Regretfully, she agreed that adoption was the best plan for the child.

Group 5: Accepts child was at risk but adoption not seen as fair and/or necessary

In this group, the birth relative identifies problems in the birth family and acknowledges that these might have had a negative impact on child. However, they argue that adoption would not have been necessary had children's services' intervention been different; for example, they may argue they needed more help, more time or that other members of the birth family should have been allowed to look after the child. Hence they do not agree with the adoption plan.

Case study: Birth mother, Sonia

Sonia became pregnant whilst in a six-year relationship and had a little girl. She moved out of the area because she was experiencing violent abuse within the community, not from her partner. She struggled to settle in a new town. She had health problems, suffering from bulimia and was diagnosed with borderline personality disorder. Sonia says that she was very mentally ill and that this was impacting on her daughter. She approached children's services for help after she smacked the child on the leg. She concedes that she could not meet the child's needs and that she was re-enacting her own upbringing. She wanted help with her parenting and does not agree with the plan for adoption. She feels that she asked for help but what she got was an "investigation".

Table 5.4 shows the numbers and percentages of birth relatives who fell into each of these five groups. The smallest group (Group 1) were birth relatives who denied any problems, and the largest group (Group 5) were the birth relatives who both acknowledged problems and accepted that the child was at risk, but did not agree with the adoption.

Table 5.4
Birth relatives' views about why their child/grandchild was adopted

	Number	*Percentage*
Group 1: Denies any problems	7	10.1
Group 2: Locates problem with other person/s	11	15.9
Group 3: Accepts problems but denies child risks	16	23.2
Group 4: Accepts concerns and supports adoption	9	13.0
Group 5: Accepts child at risk but opposed to adoption	26	37.7
Total	**69***	**99.9**

*Four couples were interviewed together. In these cases only one code per couple was assigned.

We then looked at these five groups in terms of two key dimensions: whether the person mainly agreed or disagreed with children's services' view of whether the child was harmed or at risk of harm; and whether the person acknowledged or did not acknowledge problems affecting the family. Table 5.5 cross tabulates these two dimensions and shows how the five groups fit within this framework.

According to Table 5.5, we can see that although the vast majority of relatives disagreed with the adoption plan (87%), two-thirds acknowledged family problems and agreed to some extent with children's services about the concerns for the child (67%). Only one in 10 birth relatives portrayed themselves as having no problems at all and their child as being at no risk of harm. These data suggest that it is far too simplistic to think that birth relatives in compulsory adoption cases have no insight into why their child needs to be adopted. Our data suggest that there is

Table 5.5
Birth relatives' agreement with child's adoption

	Mainly agrees with children's services' view of child harm	Mainly disagrees with children's services' view of child harm
Acknowledges problems affecting the family	Disagrees with adoption Group 5 $N = 26$ (38%) Group 2 $N = 11$ (16%) Agrees with adoption Group 4 $N = 9$ (13%)	Disagrees with adoption Group 3 $N = 16$ (23%)
Does not describe any problems	Empty	Disagrees with adoption Group 1 $N = 7$ (10%)

much variation between birth relatives on this dimension, and that it is a small minority of people who completely deny all problems. However, this is not to say that birth relatives had an understanding of the reasons why the child needed to be adopted similar to that of the professionals involved in the case. It is likely to be difficult for birth relatives to admit to all problems affecting their parenting, and even more difficult to acknowledge the full extent of their impact on their children. Denial, shame, anger and guilt may influence people's narratives and their acceptance of the adoption plan. The perspectives of other people involved in adoption – the adopted child, the professionals, the adoptive parents – are also of great relevance and importance; they are, however, not the focus of this study.

Summary

This chapter has described the characteristics of the sample of birth relatives who took part in the study. It has used qualitative data to describe the problems birth relatives experienced in parenting the child, and their feelings of agreement with or opposition to the adoption plan. Key findings are as follows:

- Seventy-three birth relatives took part in the study: 44 birth mothers, 19 birth fathers and 10 grandparents. Birth relatives were interviewed twice, and 78 per cent ($n = 57$) took part in the second round of interviews.
- Eighty-nine per cent of birth relatives were white, and 11 per cent from minority ethnic groups.
- Only 18 per cent of birth relatives were in employment. Over 40 per cent were unemployed; more than one in five were unable to work because of ill health or disability.
- Most birth parents had more than one child and were currently, and usually permanently, separated from all of their children. For 60% of birth parents, all their children had been adopted or were going to be adopted. Only four birth parents were caring for a child at the time of interview.
- Generally, the "index" adopted child had been compulsorily removed at a very young age (64% were removed under the age of one) and most people were going through the adoption process for this child at the time of the study (31.5% of children had not yet been placed for adoption at the time of first interview) or had been through this process in the last two years.
- Almost all birth parents and grandparents described more than one serious and long-standing problem that they felt had contributed to the child's entry into care and adoption. The most commonly cited problems were relationship difficulties (41%), mental health problems (33%), and substance misuse issues (32%).
- A minority of birth relatives (13%) were in agreement with the adoption plan. Most birth relatives were opposed to the adoption, although again it was only a small minority (10%) who denied any parenting problems and any claims of harm to the child. In most cases, birth relatives acknowledged parenting problems and harm to the child, although they frequently disputed the level of these problems or harm, or argued that they had received insufficient help to look after the child.

6 Birth relatives' experiences of compulsory adoption

This chapter uses qualitative data from interviews with birth relatives to describe what it is like for a parent or grandparent to lose their child or grandchild in compulsory adoption proceedings. The chapter roughly follows the chronology of events – from their immediate reactions to the removal of the child, through the process of negotiating care and adoption proceedings, and to the situation they were left with after the child was placed (usually very minimal contact with the child). We have chosen to include these experiences in some detail because it was clear, from the interviews, that the adoption process itself was significant; it was plainly not just the "outcome" of adoption (the loss of the child) that was considered important and required adjustment to, but the manner in which people felt this had occurred. The Adoption and Children Act 2002 and accompanying guidance requires that birth relatives should be supported *through* (and not just after) the adoption process and that they should be entitled to an independent worker *from the time adoption is identified as the plan*. This is another important reason to consider people's experiences before the adoption is finalised. We recognise that this data is subjective – it is the adoption story from the birth relatives' point of view. We acknowledge that there are other equally valid perspectives which may tell a very different story. We would argue, however, that a focus on the "lived experience" of birth relatives is a good starting point for understanding people's support needs.

The immediate crisis of the child's removal

Birth parents and grandparents participated in the study at different points in time in relation to the adoption. How people were dealing with the experience at the time of their interviews is considered in later chapters; this section describes the experience of birth relatives around the time of the child's removal and the adoption decision. For some this experience was current or very recent, for others it was in the past.

The child was most often removed when long-standing problems came to a head, but it was clear that, for the majority of birth relatives, this loss of the child then precipitated its own crisis. Most birth relatives described the experience using words and phrases such as "devastating", "heart-breaking", "vile", "like torture", "having your heart ripped out" or being "torn apart". These words indicate both intense personal distress and a sense of having a part of themselves physically removed; to quote Parkes' classic work on bereavement, they used 'words implying mutilation and outrage' (2001, p 98). It was common that people referred to the experience in terms of bereavement, but a bereavement without certainty or closure: 'It's worse than someone dying . . . it's worse because I don't know where they . . . I don't know who they're with, I don't know if he's getting bullied at school . . . It's just a constant stress . . .' The chain of events which followed the child's entry into care led to a range of consequent "symptoms" or reactions. Many described a period of extreme turbulence in which they experienced symptoms such as physical sickness, suicidal thoughts or attempts, confusion and disorientation, anxiety and numbness, intense anger or paranoia. The point in the adoption process which could thrust people into this state varied from person to person. For some, it was the initial removal of the child; for others, it was the failure of an assessment, or being told of the adoption decision or the last contact with the child. Intense feelings were described by grandparents as well as parents; one grandmother compared her loss of her baby grandson to a 'phantom limb', saying that sometimes she could still feel him cradled in her arms.

Almost two-thirds of birth relatives ($n = 47$, 64.4%) reported a diagnosis or symptoms of clinical depression (e.g. low mood, sleep and eating disturbances, apathy, low self-worth, hopelessness, suicidal thoughts) which, in their opinion, was triggered or exacerbated by the loss of the child. One birth father described this as follows:

> *When [my daughter] got adopted, on my last day of contact, I went to my mum's and I sat down and I never ate for two days . . . every time I tried eating something I was sick, physically sick . . . the doctor gave me . . . some Prozac and he gave me some sleeping pills, because I couldn't sleep . . . I never slept for three nights solid . . . every time I*

went to sleep, or tried to go to sleep I just had these flashbacks of [my daughter], of that particular day, the last contact . . . I was on anti-depressants for about four months . . . My mum had to come down to the doctors, because probably if I would have went down on my own . . . I wouldn't have known what I was doing. I could have walked in the middle of the road and not noticed cars going down and got knocked over, and that's how bad I was.

Depressed birth relatives often referred to feelings of low self-worth or guilt, a sense of hopelessness or helplessness, and an inability to carry on with their day-to-day life: 'We walked out of [the court] in tears.' 'We were lifeless for months.' 'I came out of my job; I knew that if I carried on I would have lost fingers or hands.' 'I felt like I had let everybody down, more so my daughters.'

Over a quarter of birth relatives ($n = 19$, 26%) felt so despairing that they had had thoughts of ending their own life and nine of these said that they had attempted to do so:

I was on self-destruct mode for a long time with a good few suicide attempts . . . all I wanted to do for a while was die. That way, if I was dead, I could at least get to watch over the girls; at least I would still get to see them that way.

A further three birth parents talked about self-harming as a response to their emotional distress:

When he first got taken away, I was stabbing myself in the chest with a fork . . . I've self-harmed in the past but not to that extent. I saw nothing in front of me . . .

Seven birth relatives specifically mentioned using drugs or alcohol to try and block out their pain at this time. For example, one birth mother who used drugs during her pregnancy said that when she realised her child was to be adopted, 'I carried on taking crack and drinking and whatever . . . I just went completely and utterly off the rails.'

Thirty-three birth relatives (45.2%) reported feeling extremely anxious and stressed, for example, one said:

There was a lot of pressure on my head, I felt like I was going to explode. I have never suffered with my nerves in all my life and then I ended up going to the doctors suffering with my nerves.

Some people described a generalised state of anxiety, sometimes accompanied by restlessness, anger, or eating and sleeping disturbances. Other people reported specific fears, usually an anxious preoccupation about the welfare of their child: 'I think of her 24 hours a day'. Fourteen people felt that psychological problems, such as depression and anxiety, had taken a toll on their physical health, causing or exacerbating problems such as high blood pressure, asthma or weight loss.

Anger was a feeling reported by many birth relatives, but in almost one-third of cases (*n* = 22, 30%) this was particularly intense, character-ised by all-consuming, often indiscriminate feelings of rage, and some-times accompanied by violent outbursts. These feelings could lead to isolation from friends and family and to behaving in a way likely to be seen by professionals as, at best, inappropriate:

When me mates came up and they mentioned kids I would jump in . . . I would slag me mouth off at them. At one time I just lost it . . . I would just jump up and have a right go at [my partner] for no reason whatsoever . . . [In court] all of a sudden I just jumped and I said, 'Look, they have taken my fucking bastarding kids off me'. I said, 'They are not going to fucking stop me from fucking seeing the kids' . . . And I just stormed out.

Some birth parents felt that losing control at these times of intense stress could permanently be held against them as future decisions were taken regarding contact and meeting of the adoptive parents:

I have threatened [the social worker] but that's only when they called me a liar and I won't get called a liar because I'm not and I'm not going to stand there and take it. I stood up for myself and ever since that day I blew it.

During this period of crisis, many birth relatives felt disorientated and confused, this disorientation being caused by mental distress, or by the uncertainty of what was going to happen next. As one birth mother put it:

> *I was in such a mess because I didn't know what was going on and it made dealing with the loss of the children very difficult . . . everything was all up in the air, it meant my emotions were all up in the air as well . . .*

It was common for people to be unable to take in information or relate to others or events appropriately for a period of time, all of which no doubt had implications for their ability to work with or accept support from others and participate in events and decisions.

Going through care and adoption proceedings

As has been seen already, most birth relatives in this study had not wanted the adoption to take place and felt much anger and resentment towards those who made the decision against their wishes. We acknowledge that people's memories and interpretations of professionals' behaviour are likely to have been coloured by anger, bitterness, resentment and/or guilt. Although these interviews cannot be assumed to be an accurate representation of professional practice, it is nevertheless vitally important to listen to how birth family members feel, to be open to learning from their insights about what is and is not seen to be fair and helpful, and to consider whether practice actually is always as good as it should be.

What is interesting when considering birth relatives' experiences of professional practice is the fact that they were able to discriminate between different events and different people. Despite the strong negative emotions that many people expressed, over half of those interviewed were able to identify what they felt to be good practice from at least one worker from their local social services department. Nearly all people were able to describe specific examples of what was liked and disliked about the way the various professionals worked with them. The following sections describe four key factors that emerge as important in understanding what is helpful (and not helpful) to birth relatives going through the compulsory adoption of their child.

Honesty, openness and integrity

Many birth relatives felt that professionals were not always open, honest or just in their handling of the case. It was common for people to express feelings of betrayal towards those who worked with them. For example, some spoke of how workers were encouraging towards them about their chances of keeping their child and they were then not prepared to suddenly be told that they could not. There were claims that new concerns about their parenting were brought up right at the end during a final meeting or in court, leaving people without an opportunity to address these issues. Some felt that social workers had held back information that should have been made clear to them, or did not tell them about meetings that they could have attended and which had turned out to be very important.

Some people spoke of receiving contradictory information from different departments or workers or even from the same worker, which led to confusion and frustration: 'At one stage they decided not to let me see him any more and then they said I could, then they said I couldn't and it was going on for two-and-a-half years'. Broken promises also led to feelings of betrayal. For example, one birth father commented: 'They were saying . . . I would still be able to have direct contact, but now . . . they've changed their opinions [saying] now we've nearly got her adopted you're not going to see her when she is adopted, it's going to be indirect contact'.

Some people felt that workers were hiding something if information was not forthcoming or events not explained: 'So I'm asking questions and not getting the proper answers and when I do get the answers I'm pretty much thinking that they're lies. Because I got no trust . . .'

For some people, feelings of distrust and betrayal could have long-lasting consequences affecting their ability to work with professionals; not just the individual they felt had let them down but others from the same team or agency. One father said: 'I don't tell social services anything . . . Not after what they've done to me. I don't tell them nothing.' It sometimes helped if birth relatives dealt with an entirely different team as the adoption progressed. Around a quarter of people were able to describe workers from the post-adoption contact team in much more positive terms. There were many comments that the post-adoption team or letterbox services were 'not the same as the others', or 'on my side'.

The adversarial nature of adoption undoubtedly makes the establish-ment of trusting relationships between parents and professionals difficult, but there were examples of where this had been successfully achieved. Reassurance could be built by workers being open and honest about difficult information, providing a written copy of all that was discussed together and providing details or evidence beyond a simple message that their child was 'fine'. For example, one birth relative described how her social worker managed being truthful without coming across as hostile: 'She was outspoken and honest with everything she said, she didn't beat about the bush or humour you . . . she was nice and polite with it.'

Availability, reliability and competence of workers

It was common for birth relatives to speak of difficulties in getting hold of social workers. People appreciated those workers who always returned their calls, encouraged contact and took immediate action when needed. Some people referred to many changes in social worker which meant dealing with people who did not know their case. One birth father noted: 'Because we had eight different social workers, every time someone came in they had to just go over it and when you're reading notes it's not the same as knowing the family, is it?' In contrast, it was usually appreciated when people could deal consistently with named workers. A birth mother said that, whenever she phoned her social worker, he was friendly, always remembering her and asking how she was.

Many concerns were raised about the youth and inexperience of social workers. Several people mentioned feeling negative about social workers who were not themselves parents:

> *The social worker . . . is about 25 years old, bearing in mind I'm 34, and she, she's got no kids, just come out of child-snatching school, and basically she's trying to patronise me saying she knows how I feel . . . she don't know jack shit about how I feel.*

Choice of worker could be important for some people. One birth father pointed out that workers were nearly always female, and this made them more difficult for him to talk to.

Frustrations were described when birth relatives were obliged to continue to deal with individuals or teams that they had difficult relations with or did not trust:

> *I wish [letterbox contact] didn't have to go through this social services thing because I don't like the thought that my one and only vague piece of contact has to be edited by "that woman" . . . it just stirs up all the bad feelings that I have towards her.*

However, there was also evidence that poor relationships could change. One birth mother spoke of how her social worker rang her up a few days after the court decision. She thought that was 'nice in one respect because they were thinking about me and, you know, realising that it is traumatic; I didn't find them as cold or anything like that. They were very sympathetic.' In other cases, it seemed that the persistence of the worker over time brought about a change in how birth relatives felt:

> *At first I didn't get on with [the social worker] . . . It did change because she was always good with keeping us up to date with everything and going to meetings . . . She was easy to talk to . . . if we wanted to know anything about the children and she would get straight back to us . . . she was really nice.*

Being kept informed, involved and consulted about events

Nearly all birth relatives felt they were not given enough information during the adoption process. Lack of information could lead to feelings of powerlessness, confusion and false expectations. One father summarised this by describing his dealings with social services as a 'cunning game', describing his sense of the power imbalance as follows:

> *I didn't know anything . . . I've never been through it before . . . it's like a football team, a professional footballers' team playing against a kids' Sunday league. There is just no contest . . . I think I could have done with a bit more support, you know, so that I was able to understand what is going, actually going on.*

Many birth relatives appeared quite confused about the different meetings, events and stages that characterise the process. Child protection conferences, planning meetings, looked after children reviews, adoption panels, court hearings – these different events could seem like a bewildering and relentless train taking them further and further away from their child. Many people spoke of being very unclear about the stage of the adoption process their child was in, not knowing about the child's placement and welfare, and not understanding what was happening about contact arrangements. A few birth relatives claimed to be unclear whether their child was still in foster care or had been adopted.

Many people were unsure what contact would be allowed, when it would start and how it would work. Around a third of birth relatives referred to periods of several months – or even a couple of years – following placement and prior to the adoption of their child where they had no information about their progress or welfare. Some people were insistent that they were simply not kept informed. In other cases, it was clear from birth relatives' own accounts that their capacity to understand, read or remember information given to them whilst the adoption process was moving along was often compromised. One mother said, 'They do explain it to me, but it's like it goes in one ear and out the other ear cause I can't keep hold of the thoughts inside. I keep forgetting, do you know what I mean?' Other people mentioned that information was given to them, but they could not really understand it: 'They used all the posh words, and that and I mean I didn't understand . . . I don't understand all these big words they use.'

One birth mother summarised well the feelings of many when she described how she felt treated and what would have helped her:

*What I would have liked . . . to really feel that I was actually import-
ant in all this, because I have been made to feel like I am not, like I
have been patronised the whole way through as if I am like . . . like I
am clueless . . . I mean I am actually her mother, I gave birth to her
and it is like I haven't had a say in anything and I have been made to
feel like I haven't got the right to have a say in anything . . .*

When birth relatives were given relevant and timely information about what was happening, this was of a great help to them. One birth mother appreciated her child's foster carer phoning every day with an update on the child's welfare. Another mother said her social worker called her once a month to provide information on events and the children's wellbeing and that she had promised to do so until six months after the children's adoption. Some people were not only provided with information but included in decision making regarding the prospective adoptive parents, and in putting together life story books and later life letters. There were some good examples of collaboration and information sharing between workers and birth relatives. For example, one birth relative described how the social worker helped her make a life story book for her child.

The identification of adoptive parents is obviously a key stage in the adoption process, and for almost all birth relatives one in which they felt they had virtually no choice or control. However, nearly half of the people in our sample did get the opportunity to meet the adoptive parents, and most of those who did so very much welcomed this opportunity. Thirty-two birth relatives said they had met the adoptive parents of their child (48.5% of those 66 whose child had been placed by Time 2). The key benefit that most people identified was to be able to picture the adoptive parents for themselves and to have a more positive view of the family their child would be brought up in. As one mother said, '[The meeting] put my mind at rest'. Other benefits were liking and feeling liked by the adoptive parents. Many people were very pleased (and sometimes surprised) to be informed by the adoptive parents that their child would be told about them, shown contact letters and told that they were loved by their birth family. Some birth relatives did not see meeting with adoptive parents as a significant form of involvement in the adoption process, but instead described the limitations and restrictions that they felt were erected by professionals. Some people felt they were held back from asking questions they were keen to know the answers to. One grandmother was allowed a short meeting with the adoptive parents but was told she could not ask anything about 'what they do' or of 'their life in general . . . I mean, the sort of stuff you need to know'. Short and restrictive meetings often left birth relatives feeling frustrated about how little they had been able to learn about the adoptive parents.

A small number ($n = 4$) of birth relatives had chosen not to meet the adoptive parents. One birth mother said, at the time of her first interview, that she didn't want to meet them because she felt a great deal of anger against them for having her daughter: 'They have got my little girl for no reason at all and I would have just told them what I thought about them . . . I would probably cause trouble with them.' Two people who had declined a meeting at the Time 1 interview, at Time 2 told us that a meeting was now being arranged. As one mother explained, she was worried that soon after the court case she would not be able to contain her feelings during a meeting, and it was very important to her that she had another opportunity to meet the adoptive parents after some time had gone by. For most people who had not met the adoptive parents, however, the opportunity to do so had not been available to them. For 28 people (42.2% of those whose children had been placed) the meeting was not allowed or arranged, although the birth relative reported in their interview that they had wanted a meeting. This was either because the adoptive parents had not wanted the meeting, children's services had not allowed it, or it just had not been arranged. In our sample as a whole, fewer birth fathers than birth mothers had met the adoptive parents (53% of mothers; 39% of fathers). A few grandparents claimed they were not given inform-ation or were told they could not meet the adoptive parents as they 'were only grandparents'. One grandparent said, 'I feel like I am proving myself all the time, like: "Oh, you are a grandparent but it's normally the parents we deal with".'

A sensitive and supportive attitude

A consistent theme in birth relatives' narratives was the recognition (or more usually lack of) by workers of the personal pain they were experien-cing as a result of their separation from the child. Many people claimed that they were offered no emotional support by their local authority around the child's removal or adoption. A term that parents and grand-parents often used to describe how they felt their local authority treated them after the adoption of their child was "dumped". One parent said:

> *They don't care once they've got them. They take the kids off us and then they stop working with us . . . After they take a child I think they should support you and they don't . . . It feels like being left sort of high and dry.*

In some cases, birth relatives felt that their reactions to the child's adoption were not looked at in context, but were taken as further evidence of their emotional instability. One birth parent described this as follows:

> *Because I was getting worse and worse, depression-wise, and anxious, they said I was unfit . . . This is what I can't understand about them . . . it's not as if I have decided to give the kids away, they were taken away from . . . I was anxious, depressed, all normal feelings when your kids have been took . . . What do they expect? Do they expect you to have a laugh?*

Some people felt that not enough care and consideration were given around important and highly emotional events such as one-off meetings with the adoptive parents or the last face-to-face contact with a child. One father described his last visit to see his daughter as indicative of (in his view) the generally unthinking, uncaring attitude of his social workers. He had a complicated journey to get there, travelling on public transport, and then had to hurry away to another long and complicated journey to a contact session with his son (who was in foster care). Some people felt their need for contact and reassurance about their child was not given significance: One father said he had a 'cold' response when asked if he could have photos of his youngest daughter: 'They got quite nasty and said, you know, "It is only by choice and we can stop this at any time".'

Birth relatives' experiences were not always negative and it was clear that many people did, at some point in the process, meet with someone who they felt took time to listen to and respect their feelings. The experience of some birth relatives demonstrate that the child care social worker could convey support and respect, even though they were pursuing the plan for adoption. For example, a birth parent couple saw one worker differently because she showed 'humanity' and 'decency': she took toiletries to the birth mother when she was in hospital, sent the birth father a sympathy card when his father died and made pre-adoption contact more enjoyable by letting them go to the park with their daughter. In other cases, it seemed that it was easier for birth relatives to see workers from outside of the child care team as being supportive. For example, one person contrasted the post-adoption social worker with others she had dealt with: 'She is a lot easier to talk to than the social workers . . . She is a really nice woman . . . she is not one of them; she is more like one of us . . .' One birth father said that the staff at the family centre where he was having contact with his daughter 'were very, very supportive towards me'.

After placement: contact issues

Involvement in contact planning and the "contact gap"

The vast majority of birth relatives had a plan for ongoing letterbox contact with the adoptive parents and/or the adopted child. These plans varied in terms of frequency (though most were once or twice a year) and whether photographs, vouchers or gifts could be included, whether the contact was one-way or two-way, and whether the child was to be involved in sending and receiving letters. Four people seemed to have no contact plan and four people had a plan for face-to-face contact. In almost every case, birth relatives felt that the involvement they had in shaping the contact plan was negligible or nonexistent, either because their wishes were ignored – 'They say that the way it's gone, is the way it's going to stay' – or because they felt there was no point in even expressing a preference: 'I ain't gonna ask them for photos when I know I ain't gonna get them'.

Contact did not seem to have been even discussed with some of those we interviewed. For some of them, the placement had not yet occurred or was imminent, but for others, placement had been made some time ago; they had received no information about how their child was getting on and did not know how to find out. For example, one birth father who had a final goodbye visit with his child six months prior to the Time 1 interview still had no information about his child when he had his second interview over a year later. He spoke of how he had given up phoning to ask about him: 'I don't know anything and I'm sick to death of asking and not finding out'. In some cases, although contact had been discussed and planned, it was not always taking place, sometimes because it had not been set, and in other cases because it had stopped.

One of the key features of the adoption process for birth relatives was the gradual reduction, and finally cessation, of face-to-face contact with their child. For many, this led to feelings of great uncertainty as to how their child was getting on and the need for more reassurance about their child's welfare was a clear theme. Not hearing how a child was getting on was often very distressing, especially for those people whose personal experiences of abuse and loss had taught them to see the world as an unsafe place. A particular issue for over a third of the sample was a long period between the final "goodbye" face-to-face contact with the child and the first contact letter. This period, which lasted from six months to over two years, was a time of much worry as to the child's welfare and lack of clarity about when contact would start. After children had been placed with adoptive parents, the once seemingly constant round of meetings, assessments and court dates stopped, and with this the contact with people who could answer questions was curtailed.

Such gaps in contact could be bridged by a trusted social worker who could liaise with the adoptive parents on the birth relative's behalf. Few people had access to such support at this time; only a couple of people described this experience:

I respected [the social worker] that much and I trusted her to find a good family . . . she kept me in touch all the time and all the way until the adoption papers were signed, even when they were with [the adoptive parents]. She was visiting them once a month and every month without fail she wrote to me telling me how they were and what they were doing.

Experiences of receiving contact letters

Once contact begins, the picture that emerges is that although contact is very much appreciated by almost all birth relatives (only one person we spoke to was happy not to have contact), taking part in contact is a complex experience, and one which many people need support with. Many people referred to mixed and intense emotions that were raised by the arrival of letters. Negative emotions included feelings of loss or sadness that they were missing seeing their child growing up: 'I cry as soon as I get the picture . . . it just hurts me, I'd like to see her swim and these things hurt'. In other cases, letters could bring up angry feelings. One father described getting a letter as like a punishment and 'a piss take' and another parent said, 'It just annoys me whenever I pick them up . . . It just makes me angry . . .'

For the vast majority of birth relatives, contact gave at least some reassurance that their child was alive and doing well. It could also give them an opportunity to delight and take pride in the child's achievements, and realise the opportunities they were having with their adoptive family. However, many birth relatives remained suspicious and unsure about the child's welfare when only letters were received without photographs. It was clear that for many people photographs were much more reassuring and could be trusted more than the written word:

> *It helps me to see the photos because I can see how the kids are. Otherwise I would be thinking, 'Well, are they lying, are the kids really OK?' But to see them in the photos, smiling and happy, you can see just looking in their eyes that they are happy.*

Birth parents and grandparents wanted not to be forgotten and for their child to know they were loved through the letters. Hence people particularly appreciated adoptive parents who made it clear that they helped the child remember his or her birth family. Pictures, drawings or words from the child themselves were really appreciated and again taken as very clear evidence of their welfare and confirmation that the adoptive parents were open and communicative about the child's birth family. Letters that were brief and formal, giving very little information about the child's feelings and character, usually gave less satisfaction, as did the lack of or poor quality photographs. Many of those having contact wanted it to be more frequent, detailed or open. Having letters only once a year made people feel they were missing out on big chunks of the child's life. Brief letters meant that they were unable to have a real feeling of how their children were. One birth parent described the content of her letters, as 'the most basic, skeletal crap'. The key issue for all birth relatives in the study was to have enough information and reassurance as to how the child was doing.

Although most people wanted more frequent and detailed contact, this was not the case for all. One birth father was happy with the brief letter which told him how his daughter was doing; he thought that the adoptive parents probably realised that more detail might be hurtful to him. Although many birth relatives would have wanted an option of face-to-face contact, there were a few who did not think they could cope with this.

Experiences of responding to contact letters

Some birth relatives clearly enjoyed writing to their child and took great care over the letter. However, many people mentioned problems they had with writing letters and a large number of these had not been given help or advice. A range of problems were referred to, including:

- **Learning or literacy difficulties**: 'I'm not one for writing letters because I can't put into words what I want to say anyway . . .'
- **Lack of clarity over the rules of the letterbox system**: 'Nobody's actually been down and told us what we're allowed to do or not.'
- **Disagreement with rules**: A specific issue here for many people was how they were allowed to sign the letters and there were different rules for different people about the signing of letters or cards. Some agencies seemed to insist on first names only, others allowed birth mothers to write "mummy" followed by their name or "tummy mummy". Some people did not know what was "allowed". Some birth relatives had strong feelings about the signing of their letters, but these varied from person to person.
- **Difficulty in finding the right words**: 'It's very hard to try and come up with something to say to your child you've not seen since a month after he was born . . . What do you say to that child? It's very hard.'
- **Uncertainty about the impact of contact on the child**: Around a quarter of birth relatives seemed very uncertain as to whether their child would be told about them or be aware of communication between the adoptive family and birth family members. Some thought that letters would confuse the child or cause more harm than good. There were a few people who were very concerned that their child would feel rejected or to blame for the separation and were desperate to have an opportunity to explain that this was not so. They therefore worried when contact was not allowed or took time to set up:

> *I think it is important especially for my eldest to know that I miss him . . . I really needed him to know that he doesn't have to worry about me and that it was OK for him to get on with his own life.*

Summary

This chapter has presented the qualitative analysis of interview data, describing how birth relatives experienced the removal of the child, the process of care and adoption proceedings, and the aftermath of adoption. Key themes emerging from this analysis are as follows:

- Having already often been in difficulty before their child's removal, many birth relatives described how the removal of the child from their family precipitated intense feelings of confusion, anger and distress, often accompanied by erratic behaviours. At exactly the time when parents needed to be most together, they often fell apart.
- Many people experienced the subsequent chain of events leading to adoption as a hostile and alienating process and one in which they had very little power to influence events.
- Four key factors emerged as important in understanding what is helpful (or in their absence, unhelpful) to birth relatives going through the adoption process. These factors were: honesty, openness and integrity; availability, reliability and competence of workers; being kept informed, involved and consulted about events; and a sensitive and supportive attitude.
- Once the child had been placed for adoption, almost all birth relatives wanted to keep in touch and most wanted more contact than the usually infrequent mediated letter contact that had been planned. For about one-third of people we talked to, there was a substantial time gap between contact with their child in care stopping and contact with the child in their adoptive family starting. During this gap, many people were unsure of when and how letter contact would take place and worries about the child were high.
- For those people whose letter contact had started, although any news of their child was welcome, receiving letters often gave rise to mixed feelings and writing letters posed both practical and emotional challenges.

7 The use of support services by birth relatives

Although almost all the birth relatives in our study were contacted via birth relative support providers, not everyone that we spoke to had used support services. People ranged widely from having received no independent support to having had regular input over a period of more than two years. This chapter explores how much and what types of support birth relatives in the study had experienced.

The amount of services birth relatives had used

Taking account of people's experiences at each point in time that we interviewed them, we devised four categories according to their use of birth relative support services:

Regular service users: People who had used the services of the agency on at least five occasions. This group included those who had used services intermittently over quite a long period of time, and those who had used the services regularly and extensively, for example, having weekly appointments over the course of a year.

Brief service users: People who had engaged with services but had received less than five sessions/meetings.

Knew about services but did not use them: People who knew about the availability of services, but, for whatever reason, had not actually used services. This group did include some people who had had an initial conversation with the service provider in which information about the service was given.

Neither used nor knew about services: People who had not had any contact with birth relative support services and who had no knowledge of the availability of services.

Table 7.1 shows that, whilst most (89%) birth relatives in our sample at least knew of the existence of birth relative support services, only two-thirds (66%) had used any services and less than half (45%) had used services regularly. There were different patterns between the three types of birth relatives in their use of services. Over 70 per cent of birth mothers had used some services as had 63 per cent of birth fathers, but most mothers using services were regular users, whereas the majority of fathers using services were brief or sporadic users. Only 40 per cent of grand-parents had used a support service but those who did so all used services regularly. Overall, 73 per cent of birth mothers had used a service compared to only 55 per cent of other relatives. However, no significant statistical association between relative type (mothers compared with non-mothers) and service use (used or not used) was found ($\chi^2 = 2.39$, $df = 1$, $p = .122$, ns).

Table 7.1
Categories of service use

	All birth relatives		Birth mothers		Birth fathers		Grandparents	
	N	%	N	%	N	%	N	%
Regular service five or more sessions)	33	45.2	24	54.5	5	26.3	4	40
Brief or sporadic (less than five sessions)	15	20.5	8	18.2	7	36.8	0	0
Know about but did not use (no sessions or introductory info only)	17	23.3	9	20.5	4	21.1	4	40
None – no services known about	8	11.0	3	6.8	3	15.8	20	20
Total	73	100	44	100	19	100	28	100

What types of support were received?

The interviews of birth relatives who had used support services briefly or regularly were analysed to determine what types of support they had received. This analysis focused on the function of the support, as described by the birth relative. The analysis takes account of the fact that in any one "meeting" or "session", the support worker may have offered more than one type of support (for example, in one session a worker may provide both counselling and advice and information), and that some support activities take place outside of direct meetings with workers (for example, the worker may contact other people on behalf of the birth relative). This functional analysis identified five different types of support service, as follows.

Support focused upon feelings and emotions (emotional support): This included mainly talking-based provision centred upon helping birth relatives to deal with feelings and emotions directly or indirectly related to the adoption of their children.

Advice/information giving and the provision of practical support: This category included support concerned with passing over knowledge and advice relating to care proceedings and the adoption process. Practical help such as providing transport to meetings was also included in this category.

Help with contact: This was concerned with support that helped the birth relative to maintain connections with their child and the adoptive family.

Advocacy and liaison: This was concerned with tasks which involved the support worker communicating with external agencies to seek information or act on the birth relative's behalf.

Agency-facilitated group and peer support: This involved enabling birth relatives to connect with other birth relatives in a similar situation to themselves.

Table 7.2 shows how many of the 48 birth relatives who received services received each of these five different types of service; this shows that emotional support was the most common type of support received and peer support the least common.

Table 7.2
Use of the five different types of services amongst those who used any service

	N	%
Emotional support	40	83.3
Advice/information	26	54.2
Help with contact	29	60.4
Advocacy and liaison	23	47.9
Group support	16	33.3

The types of services which were available and what people chose to use varied from case to case. Almost four-fifths of birth relatives who used services received more than one type of service ($n = 38$, 79%). The mean number of types of service people received was 2.8 ($sd = 1.3$). Unsurprisingly, the more types of services people used, the more likely they were to be regular service users (e.g. 45–50% of those receiving 1–2 services were regular service users compared with 100% of those who used four or five types of service).

Birth relatives' descriptions of support received from agencies

Descriptions of support focused upon feelings and emotions

One way that birth relatives received emotional support was through formal, talking-based "counselling" or "therapy" sessions. Some birth relatives had attended a regular sequence of such sessions, sometimes after being on a waiting list for some time. Different forms of counselling were offered, and some people described sessions which focused only on adoption-related issues, whilst other people explored wider concerns, for example, experiences in their past. Help with recognising and managing emotions was sometimes provided, for example, one birth mother said her counsellor had used puppets to help her understand the arguments that she had with her partner and the roles both played: 'He understands emotions and is teaching me to recognise how people's behaviour shows their emotion'. Birth relatives described how these counselling-type sessions could offer a chance to offload feelings, receive reassurance that one's feelings and emotions were normal and valid, as well as to enable shifts in thinking and perspectives. One birth mother was helped to recognise that her ex-partner (who was a key reason for the adoption of the children) would never be a good support for her. Some people described being helped to develop coping strategies to use when upset and unable to see a way forward or suggestions of things to do to cope with difficult times. For example, one birth mother said,

[My worker] told me that when it is their birthdays I should take pictures of a cake and candles and just keep it there so then one day when we meet them I can say that we celebrated your birthday.

As well as these formal sessions, many birth relatives experienced being emotionally supported by their worker in a range of informal ways. Many talked about being able to gain extra support – either in between sessions or after counselling had come to the end – by phoning to talk to the worker or dropping in to the agency base. For example, one birth mother spoke of how she could call into the agency's office at any time – she had been into the office 'a couple of times' in the last year when feeling down. One birth parent couple spoke of how they could chat with a worker when they dropped off contact cards at their support agency. They saw different workers each time but had no problem with this: 'I think we chat for about twenty minutes or a half-hour or something like that and they are helpful'. Some people were able to access emotional support at times of crisis. For example, one person said:

She's had me on the phone crying my eyes out and she's calmed me down, made me feel OK . . . I could phone her and I could tell if I had a problem, like if I thought I would go back into my old habits, I could call her.

Just having the reassurance that someone was there if needed was experienced by some as emotionally supportive: 'If we need her, we know she's just on the other end of the phone and she'll phone us back . . .'

Some birth relatives described how informal emotional support would be initiated by their worker. One birth mother spoke of how her worker phoned from time to time to check that she was OK, offered to be present throughout and after the final goodbye visit with her child, and then visited her at her home a few days later to see how she was. A few workers who came on board at an early stage of the adoption process offered to come to the birth relatives' last contact with their child. Others gave emotional support during court hearings:

> *I have been to court three times and twice without any support, no family, I felt like I was a nobody and I felt myself being run right over . . . [my support worker] was a good support during court . . .*

Descriptions of advice/information giving and the provision of practical support

Included under this heading were support activities focused on the receipt of advice and information relating to care proceedings, the adoption process and other features of birth relatives' situations. Birth relatives spoke of how their workers answered their general questions, informed them of their rights, options and services available to them, and passed on suggestions as to what they could do to improve their situation. Specific examples of such provision included: offering insight into the assessments that people go through before being accepted as adoptive parents; outlining a typical letterbox contact system; explaining how a birth relative could make his details available for his child to contact him when older. One birth mother spoke of how her support agency had told her that meeting adoptive parents was a possibility; her social worker had not mentioned this and she was able to instigate a meeting. A birth parent couple were given the suggestion that they place tapes and letters with a solicitor for their son to receive when he was an adult. Some advice was related to struggles or hopes to parent new or future children. A birth parent struggling to parent her newborn son was given advice on how to deal with children's services in relation to her new situation. Another parent similarly spoke of how her support worker:

> ... *explained to me that if me and [my partner] ... prove to them that we have changed our lifestyles and the violence in the house, then we can prove to them that we can care and look after a child ...*

Advice and information provision were not necessarily confined to adoption specific topics; for those with children in foster care, support workers were sometimes able to shed light on systems and procedures relevant to these children, such as information about the review process. Those struggling with wider everyday issues (e.g. housing or benefits) were sometimes helped with problems in these areas.

Practical aid was also included in this category. A common form of practical assistance was the provision of transport to enable people to attend support sessions or other meetings and events related to the adoption process (such as meeting the adoptive parents). Other examples included a birth mother in prison being sent a notebook to help her keep a diary for her son and stamps so that she could contact social workers involved in her case. Another birth parent was given help with sorting out her adoption-related paperwork: 'Getting all the letters in folders from the children with folders for each child ... the letters about the court proceedings and everything else ...'

Descriptions of services that facilitated communication with children and their new families (help with contact)

The most common form of help in this category was assistance with letter-writing. This could involve the simple passing on of a template for a letter as a guide or a reference or more specific help with the phrasing and content of the letters: 'She helped me with what to put down and I just copied it all out; I know what to write but I need help with wording it'. Some people were given help with the actual writing of the letter, perhaps due to problems with reading and writing or a desire to make it as well presented as possible. For example, one birth parent said:

> *I can't read and I can't write unless [my support worker] is here; I am not good at spelling, so she wrote it and we copied it and sent it off cause I'm dyslexic so I do need the help.*

In some cases, people received help with producing letters on the computer: 'She helped us to balance the letters out and roughly what to say and also did it on the computer and printed it off'. Appointments could be made at the time each contact was due or birth relatives would call as required – sometimes receiving help over the phone. Some people needed help only with the first letters. Many were keen to actually write the letter in their own words but still found support useful in terms of checking to see whether the letter would meet with the rules and requirements, thus avoiding the pain of having it sent back. Some support workers had creative suggestions to help birth relatives with their contact dilemmas. One worker gave advice concerning the sending of birthday cards: 'I asked how I get cheap cards and she said, "Make them". So she brought one in and she showed me how she had made them and that gave me the idea of doing it.' Help with all forms of written material could be provided directly or over the phone or via the post. As shown earlier, the difficulties people had with contact could be immense and many people told us they could not have written without such help. One spoke of the encouraging role of her support worker in helping her move forward with contact: 'I was stuck'.

Quite a few birth relatives had help with producing later life letters and life story work. One birth parent couple were helped to prepare a later life letter for the children explaining why they were adopted – the worker suggested phrases and what kinds of things to include. A birth mother spoke of how her worker was helping her with 'the photos and everything, choosing them and putting them in their life story books . . . She takes them straight to the social worker.' Another birth mother said her support worker was going to help her make a video of herself for the children. Also included in this category was help with communicating directly with adoptive parents, e.g. preparing questions to ask adoptive parents at a meeting, or attending such a meeting with a birth relative to help them ask the questions they wanted to ask. One birth mother described her need for this type of service, saying that, during her meeting with adoptive parents, her support worker asked pre-prepared questions on her behalf as she could 'hardly speak' herself.

Descriptions of advocacy and liaison services

Common examples of the help people received in this category were the support workers' communication and liaison with other agencies in order to obtain case specific information on behalf of the birth relative. For example, some people said their support worker had been able to find out from social services what stage of the adoption process had been reached or obtain an update on the child's welfare. A birth father who had not had a chance to meet the adoptive parent of his child said that his support worker had been able to glean some basic information about them on his behalf. Another birth parent received an explanation of why a closed adoption was thought to be best for her children.

Support in this category could also include assisting birth relatives with their communication with external agencies, helping them to use appropriate methods and expressions to the best effect. One birth mother was helped to write a letter to an adoption panel explaining what kind of adoptive parents she would like for her children. Another spoke of how her support worker showed her which form she needed to obtain access to her file and helped her to fill it out and send it off. Another commented: 'In the beginning it was hard to talk to social services and she would talk to them about things I couldn't get across to them'. Some birth relatives wanted their support worker to deal with other authorities on their behalf because they felt there was more chance of the desired result being achieved. As one person said, 'I think they listen to her more than me'. Other birth relatives felt so bitter towards social services that they found it very difficult to have any contact with them, and so to have a third party involved was really valued.

In several cases, birth relatives described how support workers accompanied them to meetings with social workers and other professionals. One birth mother who could not read or write was joined by her support worker at case conferences. Another birth mother said her support worker organised and attended a meeting with social services to discuss the changes she would need to make in order to be able to keep any future children. Another birth mother told us her support worker came to court hearings with her and also pushed her to make sure she kept all her appointments with social services.

Several birth relatives described how their support worker had contacted the agency managing letterbox contact to clarify the contact plans or boundaries or to try and get the plan up and running. For example, one birth parent said:

> *I was trying to get in touch with the [adoption] team to see what I can and can't put in the letter and they just said they would get back to me and they never got back to me, so [my support worker] got on to them and found out what I could and couldn't put in.*

There were also many cases where birth relatives said their support worker had liaised with social services to sort out problems with the contact such as late or missing letters. One couple said their support worker had arranged for a social worker to come out to make a photo album with them. In a few cases, birth relatives said their support worker had been able to press the placing agency to set up a meeting with adoptive parents. In some cases, liaison and advocacy work could go beyond adoption-related tasks, for instance, one young birth mother in prison was helped to get a solicitor for her parole and had been offered help with her life after prison.

Descriptions of peer and group support

Several birth relatives had taken up agency-initiated opportunities to attend group support meetings with people who had been through similar experiences. Usually these groups operated at regular weekly or monthly intervals. Some groups were for a fixed period of time with a small set group of people and others were open-ended, taking place on a more indefinite basis with people joining and leaving as they wished. Some birth relatives had attended agency-facilitated social events, such as day trips with other members of the group. One birth mother spoke of how she met with four other birth mothers over a 12-week period, which finished with a party at the end. Another described her group as:

> *Very open . . . [The worker] lets us do the talking, basically. She's just there if we need her but it's us that chairs it. We all talk about our situations, what we've been doing over the month. She works round the group and we all get a chance to speak but that's the only thing*

she does do . . . they've paid for a coach to [the beach] this month . . .
We're open, we've got nothing to hide and we'll help each other . . .

Although most groups seemed to primarily involve discussion of feelings and issues with peers, providing emotional support, information, advice and feedback, some people described attending groups with more specific functions. For example, one birth mother described a group which met in the traditional way for several sessions and which then moved on to a second phase with a support worker facilitating members to do life story books for their children together. Some birth mothers had attended a group in their prison setting. In some cases, birth relatives felt that attending a group had given them access to informal support and social activities via the friendships that had developed.

One birth mother said her support agency had provided an annual activity day for birth relatives which included discussion, pampering sessions and creative activities: 'We do head massage and we make cards as well and we all got a cup last time with different fruits on it'. There was one example of peer support provision outside of a group setting for a birth mother about to be released from prison:

[My support worker] is setting up some visits for me with a woman out there whose kids have been adopted . . . she has had a bad life and that but she hasn't been in jail, but she has changed her life.

Summary

This chapter has reported on how many birth relatives in our interview sample had used support services, and what type of services they had received. Key findings were as follows:

- Two-thirds of birth relatives interviewed (66%) had used birth relatives support services. Just under a quarter of birth relatives (23%) knew that services were available but had not used any. About one in 10 birth relatives (11%) did not know that any birth relative support services were available to them.
- Of those birth relatives who had used a support service, 69% had

received five or more sessions, and we categorised these people as "regular" service users. Thirty-one per cent of people had received less than five sessions; this group were described as "brief or sporadic" service users.

- Birth mothers were most likely to have used services (73% had done so), and grandparents were least likely (only 40% had used services). Sixty-three per cent of birth fathers had used services.
- All of the grandparents (four) who had used services were regular users, as were three-quarters of birth mothers (75%). Only a minority of birth fathers (42%) using services had received five or more sessions.
- The types of services people had received were coded into five categories based on the function of the support service. The five types of support and the percentages of people using services who had received these were: emotional support (83%); advice, information and practical support (54%); help with contact (60%); advocacy and liaison (48%); group or peer support (33%).
- Most people received more than one type of support – the average was 2.8 types.

8   Birth relatives' evaluations of using support services

This chapter draws on the interviews with birth relatives who had used adoption support services. Categorical ratings of people's overall levels of satisfaction with support services are described, and key themes relating to aspects of the support service which birth relatives valued or did not value, are explored.

Birth relatives' levels of satisfaction with support services

Taking account of both of the interviews (or just the first interview for those who did not take part at Time 2), each person's level of overall satisfaction with services was coded as *primarily positive*, *mixed or neutral* or *primarily negative*, as follows.

Cases where positive comments about the service clearly outweighed negative comments were categorised as *primarily positive*. Case examples of birth relatives in this category are given below.

> *[The support] has been very, very valuable, it has helped me get stronger . . . It has helped me sort things out in my head . . . it has helped me put things in perspective . . . she has covered everything. [Without her] I don't think I would have moved on as quickly as I have.*

> *It's been good, it's been brilliant, I couldn't have done it without [my support worker] . . . she's been brilliant . . . I look on her as a friend.*

> *I'd recommend them to anybody . . . They have helped me deal with it. If it wasn't for them I don't think I would have dealt with it, I don't think I would have coped and I don't think I would have been able to move on – they have helped me move on.*

People who made a fairly equal number of positive and negative comments, or just spoke neutrally (feeling neither negative nor positive) about the adoption support received were classed as having *mixed or neutral* feelings about the service. An example of someone in this category is given below.

> *She was very nice, yes. I found that I could talk to her and she would listen to what I had to say and I got more information from her than I had from the social worker . . . They were very friendly, very welcoming and made you a cup of tea, yeah, they were very good . . . It was helpful, yes . . . but it would have been better for me if they weren't social workers . . . I think it would help if those people that were dealing with it had actually been in the situation them-selves . . . You can only understand it if it has happened to you, you then can be more understanding and actually more helpful . . . They only have one full-time lady and the lady that was helping me, she is only there part-time. Not good when you want to see somebody immediately.*

Birth relatives who made no or almost no positive comments about the support they received from the support service and who mainly referred to negative aspects of the service were coded as *primarily negative*. A case example is given below.

> *I don't want her in my life; I think she is a burden on me by coming to my house. I can write my own letter . . . What you need to do at the end of the day [is] get on with your life . . . They are not doing anything that's good for people . . . She just made me mad when she used to come . . . She just stresses me out and I can do without it . . .*

Table 8.1 shows the numbers of people who fell into each of these three categories. This illustrates that very few birth relatives reported negative experiences of using services – almost three-quarters of people were very positive.

Table 8.1
Satisfaction with support services

	Frequency	*Percentage*
Primarily positive	35	72.9
Mixed or neutral	10	20.8
Primarily negative	3	6.3
Total	**48**	**100.0**

What features of support were valued by birth relatives?

In examining what birth relatives said about what they liked or did not like about the services they had received, three overlapping themes emerged as important dimensions of the quality of support: the quality of relationship with the worker; confidentiality and independence; and a flexible and pro-active approach. The following section explores these themes and also includes information about what people liked or did not like about peer support.

The personal qualities of the worker: relationship-based support

It was clear from the accounts of almost all birth relatives that the personal qualities (skills, attitudes, values) of the support worker were an important, if not the most important, determinant of whether they were satisfied with the service or not. Birth relatives often talked of feeling that they were welcomed, accepted, respected, understood and genuinely cared about by their support worker. What workers were clearly offering was a relationship-based service, and for many birth relatives this relationship was what helped them to cope and, in some cases, change. Many people described experiencing this therapeutic alliance as something quali-tatively different to other relationships they had had with other professionals at this time in their lives: '[They were] totally different and understanding'.

Because of the reluctance and anxieties that many people felt when first approaching or being approached by support services, first impressions of the worker or agency seemed important, as the following birth parent describes:

Personally, I didn't think anybody could help me with the way I was feeling. But when I actually phoned them, they sounded lovely . . . I felt a bad person 'cos I'd lost my son . . . and I thought do they think the same? . . . And when I spoke to them on the phone, there was no judging or anything there in their voices. And I made an appointment to see them and the first time I met them, they was so accommodating, it was great, it was really helpful. I thought, yeah, I can do this.

As in the example above, it was common for birth relatives to mention the positive and accepting attitude of workers towards them. Workers were described as being non-judgmental, treating birth parents and grandparents as equals, and valuing them for who they were. One birth father commented, 'She didn't speak to me like I was a child'. Others spoke of being placed at the centre of attention, or being talked *to* and not *at*: 'They just sit there and talk to you, ask you what's the matter . . . It felt like somebody wanted to know me, to help me . . . and don't treat you like a piece of shit.' Such attitudes could give a needed boost to a shattered self-esteem. A young birth mother commented on how her worker 'kind of encouraged me to be me . . . it felt like someone actually thought that I could do better . . . she would talk to me and I wouldn't feel like trash . . . they did help me pick myself up.' Another birth mother who had made a suicide attempt, following her children's removal, spoke of how her support worker's attitude towards her made a radical difference to her life:

[My support worker was] the first person I had ever spoken to about losing the children, who listened, who didn't judge, who didn't assume that because I had lost my children I was a bad person. She understood that just because physically and emotionally I wasn't capable of looking after my children it didn't mean I didn't love them, she gave me back the most important thing that I had lost and that was self-respect . . .

This non-judgmental attitude was often set in contrast to previous inter-actions with social workers and other professionals, as one person said, 'Social services judge you, the counsellors don't judge you'. For many birth relatives, the meeting with the support worker was the first time they met someone who they felt was on their side:

> *She seemed . . . more understanding from the mother's point of view that was getting their kids took for adoption . . . It felt good for somebody like her to be supportive of what I was saying and she believed what I was saying.*

Birth relatives also spoke positively of their workers' ability to listen to and understand their feelings. One birth mother felt her worker's experience with other birth mothers enabled her to empathise: 'I knew she was there and I knew that she knew what it felt like because . . . she has seen it with other birth mothers so she knew exactly how I felt.' Many people felt there was a value in speaking to someone who was not shocked that their child had been adopted and who understood why these things happened. In some cases, people felt that the support worker was the first person they had been able to speak to about what had happened: 'That's the first time that I could have talked to anybody . . . When I had my first meeting with [her] I felt a lot had got off my chest.' For some people, there was no opportunity to talk about such issues with anyone else:

> *It is someone to talk to because I can't talk to my husband because he gets upset, I can't talk to complete strangers; I couldn't talk to any-body about it, it wasn't a normal situation at all, so it was all bottling up in me really and it was just a relief to go somewhere and talk to somebody.*

One birth father noted how he felt free to say whatever he liked in the session with his worker, especially all his angry feelings about his social worker. The worker gave him a sense of entitlement to his feelings, although strongly advised him not to act on them.

Many felt there were clear benefits from such opportunities to talk within a supportive relationship: 'When I talk to [my support worker], it helps me through, well, it's just something that relaxes my mind and what have you, I mean it helps me a bit to deal with it, you know.' One birth father felt that talking about the adoption had helped him to see things differently and deal with what had happened:

> *He listened to me and a lot of things I never spoke to anybody about, the death of my father and this, that and the other . . . The more I talk about it the better I feel. I feel that that's another bit of it dealt with . . . the more times that you talk about a problem with anybody, the more times you make that noise, the better things feel and you can understand more from it.*

Several people described how their support worker made them feel that their feelings were normal and valid:

> *The first few times we met she must have got so sick of me because all I did was rant about social services . . . but she would say 'Oh yes, I have heard that' or 'I have had a woman go through a similar thing'. And she made me realise it wasn't all in my head . . . knowing that you are not the only person that has been through that starts to make you believe that it might not be all my fault and that is a very big turning point.*

A grandmother was helped to see that she needed a grieving period and that she should not be hard on herself for getting behind with her jobs. It seemed important to many people that their support worker showed expertise in relation to adoption. Birth parents and grandparents appreciated workers who always had the answer to a problem or would find out by the next appointment. One birth father valued his worker being '. . . obviously clued up . . . she knows what she's talking about . . . She's not a young lass out of school or a trainee.' Another birth father felt he could trust advice because the worker had been 'doing this for years'.

Many people also spoke of feeling genuinely cared about by their support worker. Some referred to simple actions such as being offered a coffee, having their coat taken, being seen in nice homely surroundings, and being given time, as evidence of the support worker's care and concern. One birth mother who experienced a "pamper day" for birth relatives commented how, 'It really made you feel like a princess for the day; you know, being spoilt – it was lovely'. Care that went beyond the sessions was sometimes shown through actions such as sending cards and phoning regularly. There was generally a great appreciation of workers who would phone from time to time to check they were OK, as the following birth mother's experience shows:

It is good . . . knowing that she still does actually think about you. [My support worker] still checks how I am, I will get a text message or a phone call, like just before Christmas: 'Happy Christmas, and are you OK?' And she found out I had left [my partner] and made a phone call then to see if I was alright and just asking about my life in general and telling me that she is proud of me, and I can't remember ever hearing these words before.

Workers who were felt to have given more than expected and helped the birth relative with wider tasks and concerns were particularly appreciated and seen as genuinely caring as opposed to just doing their job. A birth mother in prison spoke of how her support worker was making her a CD of relaxing songs. Another birth mother who had passed on to her support worker the one tiny photograph she had of her grandfather, to whom she had been extremely close, for the purpose of getting it copied for the life story book, was thrilled to find her worker not only had an enlargement done for the life story book, but also had an extra enlargement done for her to keep herself: 'Just her putting a little personal bit into it that was above and beyond: she didn't have to do that, it wasn't part of her job but it is great and I don't have the worry of losing the only photograph I have ever had of him and I also have a big photograph in a frame which I love . . .' A birth father talked of how his worker 'got on the computer, in her own time, and found out some names, like [my partner's] possible real father.'

Overall, the majority of people felt they got on very well with their support worker, saying things like, 'You couldn't ask to talk to a nicer person'; 'Brilliant . . . the best person ever . . . a real diamond'. Several birth relatives said that they felt their worker was on their level, and in some cases, like a friend. One birth father said: 'He does the same things as I do and he's interested in the same things as I am, and it makes it easier for me to talk to him. I feel more comfortable with him; he talks to me on a friendly basis . . . I liked his casual dress. He wasn't a suit and tie person. He wasn't an authority figure. He could have almost been like one of my friends.' The following birth mother appreciated her worker sharing some aspects of her own life; this made the relationship feel more personal:

> *She was really nice to talk to and I got on really well with her . . . she come across really, really friendly, like somebody you had known for ages, not somebody that you had just met. I know she is professional but she was like my friend . . . She sent me little cards and that. She tells us about her life . . . we quite often have conversations where we are not even talking adoption or the boys or anything, we are just having a chat.*

Having the continuity of seeing the same person helped good relationships to develop, as one birth father said: 'You build up a rapport with someone when you've seen 'em quite a few times'. The flipside of this was that, for some people, their worker leaving was a great disappointment. One birth mother referred to feeling let down and abandoned when told by her support worker that she was changing jobs: 'She didn't bother referring me to someone else . . . now I don't know who to contact . . . I feel that at the end of the day I put in the work but nobody is giving me nothing back and I just feel like quitting.' For some people, it took time before they felt able to build a relationship with their support worker and, in some cases, people appreciated their worker's sensitivity in not pushing or questioning at the start, but slowly working to establish trust. For example, one birth mother started talking to her worker about life story work and contact, and only then, as she came to trust her, began to talk about her drug use and why her children were taken away. One birth mother described how her support worker gave her copies of her case records of all their meetings, a practice she found reassuring and which helped her to trust.

It was very rare that birth relatives criticised an individual support worker. However, there were two birth relatives who felt that their support worker could not really understand what it was like for them to have lost a child to adoption. One of them said, 'At the end of the day, it's not their children, they can't imagine what you go through. It's horrible, nobody will ever know until it happens to them.' A few people mentioned that they would have preferred support from someone who had been through a similar experience themselves.

Some people had a clear preference about the type of person they could work with, for example, their age, gender or ethnicity. One birth mother was happy when her worker changed:

> The other one was too mumsie and I had a bad experience with my mum and [the new one] was a bit older and so I found her quite helpful . . . I had a better relationship with my gran than I did with my mum . . . [She] was a lot older and a lot wiser and that's what I needed.

A few people expressed a preference for the support worker not to be a social worker, or even that, ideally, they should be a birth parent themselves who would know what it was like to lose a child. Two people would have preferred a worker of a different gender. One male interviewee who saw a female worker felt he would find it easier to talk to another man. One birth mother who saw a male worker admitted she found it difficult to confide in men due to abuse in her past. Another birth mother noted that she would not have seen a male worker and so was pleased that she was allocated a woman.

Confidentiality and independence of the service

A number of birth relatives raised issues about the confidentiality and independence of the adoption support service. Many of those who were positive about support services mentioned independence as a positive factor and several of those who were mixed or negative raised concerns about whether services actually were independent. Many birth relatives reported feeling nervous at first that everything they said to the support worker would be relayed back to the children's services team in their local authority, but in most cases people were quickly reassured about this.

Some birth relatives said that it was very important to them that their support worker was not a social worker (or employed by social services):

'Oh God no, I couldn't talk to another one; I don't trust social services'. Many (but not all) claimed that they would not have used a support service if it had been connected to social services: 'I couldn't talk to the social workers, because it were them, their fault it had gone this way'. This reluctance to have any dealing with social services seemed particularly evident when the plan for adoption had not been finalised; people feared their vulnerabilities could be exposed and used as evidence against them. For example, one birth father said:

> *If I felt really down and anxious I wouldn't have dared tell social services, because they'd say I'm being unpredictable, I can't control my emotions and I'd be scared they wouldn't let me see my kids that week or I'm not fit to look after them. Where if I said that to this adoption [support worker], she'd probably think like me, like most people, that it's normal to feel like that if your kids have been taken away.*

Some people indicated that they would have refused the service even if a social worker had merely recommended the independent adoption service or used a social services venue, as one person said, 'I think that if it was a social worker building I don't think any of us would have gone'. For a few people it was important that their worker did not even have a social work background: 'I don't think I could trust her otherwise'. A couple of people were concerned upon discovering that their support worker was a qualified social worker, as a connection to social services was then assumed. However, one person spoke of how her worker had moved away from her role as social worker: 'She is no longer part of those people, even though she might have been a part of somebody else's child getting taken away, it's like she is not working there no more'.

Even though most support received by birth relatives in the study was provided by adoption support agencies or voluntary adoption agencies, not all birth relatives were able to feel confident that their support agency was truly independent from social services; a few people seemed to view support providers as 'all in with the system'. There were six people who expressed specific concerns about the independence of their support service or who had concerns about confidentiality. In one case, the support worker was employed by the local authority but in the five other cases this was not so. However, there could still be a feeling that they were 'working for the same people'. Some people had the feeling that what they told the support worker had been reported or might be reported to social services, as the following birth mother described: 'I know for a fact that she has gone back and told social services because before I had the final contact with my last child the social worker practically told me word for word what I had said to the other lady. Now I just think that is not fair at all.' One person commented on the fact that her support service was run by a voluntary adoption agency which placed children for adoption. This only confirmed to her that they were inevitably biased and she saw getting support from them as like 'going to the pub for an alcoholics meeting'. She felt that this support service was only willing to help her if she agreed to the adoption.

A flexible and proactive approach

From birth relatives' accounts, it seemed that some agencies or workers were more flexible than others in terms of what and how much support was offered. Some people described receiving a fairly rigid structure of sessions with planned frequencies for a set period. Other people had access to a more flexible and open-ended service where support could be accessed on an "on demand" basis, and this model of delivery seemed particularly appreciated. As one birth mother explained:

> I have phoned her a couple of times . . . she's had me on the phone crying my eyes out and she's calmed me down, made me feel OK; if I need her, she is there. If we need her, then we've only got to phone her and she'll talk on the phone or come and see you at your house.

Many people described being offered open-ended help and being able to call in the future as and when needed. This offer was frequently taken up, especially around contact meetings. The number of sessions, or amount of time over which services could be used, also varied from person to person. Having flexibility about the length of time over which support could be accessed seemed to allow workers to go at the birth relative's speed. One birth mother commented:

She did everything very slowly and she took it at my pace, I mean there was a slight time restraint on it because she only had funding for so long, but I think we had something like 18 months to two years, so it was a decent amount of time.

One person appreciated that her worker did not have to stick rigidly to the 'therapeutic hour' but would stay longer if she felt more time was needed: 'However long it takes, sometimes it's an hour, and sometimes it can be longer; it just depends on how long it takes'. Another birth parent couple spoke of how their worker stayed for one-and-a-half hours, more than they'd had from a social worker in three years.

Some birth relatives felt the service available to them was too restricted in terms of the amount of support available. One birth mother who had only two sessions altogether would have liked more regular, on-demand meetings. Another also spoke of wishing her worker was contact-able between appointments. Another mentioned that her support agency had only had two members of staff so she could not always get hold of them: if something happened on Friday there would be no one available until the following Wednesday. A few people had a clear sense that their service was time-limited; for example, one person said she was allowed six sessions and that 'if you miss one you get less'. Some people described how they did have the option to apply for more sessions, but that this meant a delay until the request was agreed. Two birth mothers would have liked their support group to run for longer than the 12 weeks that had been planned. One birth mother was "gutted" when told she could no longer get help from her adoption support service or attend a support group because her local authority would not fund any further provision.

Many, but not all, birth relatives said that the agency offered flexibility around the venue/location for support to take place. Some birth relatives had talked about the difficulties they had in travelling due to costs or other problems. An opportunity to see their worker at home could mean that receiving support became possible:

Most of the time she would come and see me at home . . . that was great at the time because I was still having problems with depression

*and I suffered from very bad anxiety and I felt that it was quite difficult
to go out . . . it was easier for me to see her in an environment where
I felt safe.*

For others it just helped the session to be more relaxing: 'If you are at
home, you feel more relaxed . . . in an office you feel all uptight and all
that'. Although many people liked home visits, one birth mother felt it
was an "invasion". She appreciated instead the option of being able to
phone the agency worker to get help with contact letters.

There could also be flexibility with regard to what support was
provided, and some people stressed the importance of workers responding
to a range of needs, both practical and emotional. Some felt their workers
would help in any way needed, addressing issues beyond adoption. For
example, one person said:

*They was there. It wasn't just for the adoption. It was to see what had
gone on in my life as well, and my background . . . It was just up to
me, what I wanted to say . . . that was nice to have, not just someone
who was constantly obsessed with adoption, she realised I had other
things in my life and other things to talk about . . . if I needed
anything, I think she would have sorted it out for me.*

In contrast, there were some birth relatives who described being able to
access only one type of help, and this was usually a counselling-based
model of emotional support. While this did meet some people's needs, not
everyone was ready or able to appreciate this type of help. This was
particularly the case for a number of people in the study who were focused
upon the fight to get their children back and were only, or primarily,
interested in help that could benefit them in this area. For this group, it
was vital that their support worker could provide more than just emotional
support – they wanted information about their rights and action-based
support which would give them a sense of *doing* something. "Support" for
them was activities which challenged the adoption rather than helped
them to accept it. One birth mother expressed this as follows:

*They know what social services is doing to people: get something
done about it, don't sit and twiddle their fingers and say we can't do*

125

anything . . . it is all about trying to help people forget what has happened when really there should be action: it is just sitting there and chatting. It's no good sitting there and chatting, you need to be getting something done.

Another person felt her counsellor was not knowledgeable about her rights in fighting the adoption and therefore 'didn't know her own job'.

Of the five different types of support that birth relatives described, there did not seem to be one type that emerged as being "the best" for all people. What did seem to be important, however, was that the individual needs of each birth relative could be responded to; for those who could not face counselling, advice or advocacy needed to be available; for those who could not cope in a group, individual work needed to be offered; for those who could not travel, home visits were required; and so on. Where the service that was on offer did not match with the person's perceived need, dissatisfaction followed. For example, some people expressed dissatisfaction with workers who wanted to discuss their feelings about the adoption or topics related to their past which they did not want to think about. Conversely, there were also cases where the birth relatives wanted to talk about their feelings and they felt they were not given the opportunity to do this as the focus of their sessions was on contact. One birth father was keen for answers as to why his girls were adopted and he felt the support he was offered did not address these concerns:

We just want someone to answer questions but there isn't anyone to do that, there isn't any help. [The counsellor] has got all his questions mapped out beforehand . . . bringing up a lot of stuff that we'd put to rest years ago about our childhood. We didn't want to talk about our childhood. I wanted to know how we were going to fix what had happened . . . how we could go about fixing that and making ourselves better people.

Another birth father who was particularly keen to have a meeting set up with the adoptive parents of his girls said he 'kept pressing and pressing for that but actually nothing came of it, did it?' He could not appreciate the counselling and space to talk that he was offered:

All you are doing is constantly going over it and you are re-acting it and I am not up for this psycho-babble crap . . . sometimes it is just better to leave things alone . . . The one thing she could have done . . . she could have set up this meeting [with the adoptive parents] but nothing happened with it, because everyone was on about my needing to move on.

Another birth father spoke negatively of the help he received with letter contact because:

I just wanted to put it in my words and my feelings, but when you read the letter back it is like I come from a public school, it is not normal speak . . . it is not how I speak. I think the . . . emotion of how I feel should be in that letter, not how somebody else wants it to be.

The issue of the importance of service provision matching personal needs and preferences is clearly illustrated when people's experiences of receiving group support are examined. One-third of birth relatives who had used support services had attended a support group. People's feelings about the usefulness or otherwise of this type of support were quite varied. Some people were really positive about group support, emphasising the value of being with people who had shared the same experience – 'We're all in the same boat and we can share our feelings' – and being able to help each other, and of having the opportunity to make friends and develop social links.

I've got friends at the meetings – I call them my friends . . . I like to go because it's my day out amongst friends and we arrange things, we are going out for a meal and a drink in December for the Christmas holidays . . . I have got to know all those people now . . . It feels good going there now.

However, other people emphasised their difference from other group members. For example, one birth mother felt she did not fit in with other group members, many of whom had learning difficulties: 'We felt really let down, as though we'd been classed just like these other people and it really hurt me and I'm not going back to it'. Another birth mother had a fight with a woman from her group whom she thought was a sex offender: 'I thought, I am in a room with a bunch of paedophiles . . . I thought to myself that I know that I have a child that has been adopted, but I am nowhere near as bad as most of this lot here . . . a bunch of nutters.' Of those birth relatives who had not had the option of attending a group, some people felt this would have been helpful, for example, one person said, 'I would like to have seen some kind of people, especially those people like us who has gone through the whole system...' But other people felt that group support was not for them:

> You're sitting there in front of people that you don't even know, do you know what I mean? And you're telling them your business and I don't like doing that; I don't want to hear everyone's stories. I could also meet someone who isn't moving on and that could prevent me from moving on. I am supposed to go to a group but I don't do well in groups, I am not a group person at all.

For many people, it seemed important that service providers were assertive in following up referrals and attempting to convince people to use services, and agencies and workers seemed to differ in the extent to which they did this. Some people described workers who 'made the running' in getting them to use services, whereas other people said that they were left to take the initiative. It was clear that some birth relatives would not have initiated help for many varied reasons (such as feelings of unworthiness, depression, passivity, blocking out, a feeling that nothing could be done to help them), and only a worker willing to actively pursue them ensured they received a service. One birth mother explained how her drug worker arranged for an independent adoption support worker to visit her at home. However, when the worker knocked on her door, the birth mother was in a very poor state and high on drugs, so she escaped out of the back door. Some time later, the worker found out she was in prison and came to see her there. The mother only then agreed to her visit just to get away from the other prisoners, but this turned out to be the beginning of a fruitful working relationship. Another birth mother also commented on how her worker persevered with her 'like a dog with a bone . . . it took a lot of perseverance on her part'. The comments of some birth relatives suggested that it is helpful if workers try again, even when help is initially refused. As one person said, 'If I said I don't want to talk right now, I might not want to talk. But there's nothing to say I won't want to talk later on or tomorrow.'

It was rare for people not to appreciate efforts that workers made to contact them and offer help. The vast majority saw it as a sign of care and concern, giving them the opportunity to engage as soon as they felt ready. One birth mother who was not keen to see a support worker at the beginning described how the worker kept dropping notes regularly through her door. She felt this showed her that this person really cared about her situation and this prompted her to engage with the support offered. Only one birth relative reacted against an agency's proactive approach. This person had been angry with the worker for coming to her house, and felt she should just be left to get on with her life without interference or being made to talk about everything all over again. She did not trust professionals and felt bothered by letters inviting her to support meetings: 'I can do without it . . . I don't want those sort of people in my life. I don't trust people no more.'

There were several cases where workers had not been proactive at keeping in touch. Some people who had received just one visit from a support worker seemed to be left very much in need of (and wanting) more regular support but were unclear as to whether the worker was coming back. One birth father said that the support agency was supposed to get in touch with him for another appointment and to help him with letters but they had not done so: 'I'm waiting for them to write to me. You know, I can't see why I should have to write to them.' It was hard for some people to initiate contact with their support worker. One birth mother, for example, said that she did not feel her problems were always worth troubling her support worker with. She was told she could phone her worker if she ever had any questions or problems but said she was reluctant to do so: 'I don't like disturbing her . . . I like to try and sort it out first by myself, and then if I can't, then phone [her].'

Summary

This chapter has explored birth relatives' levels of satisfaction with adoption support services. Themes associated with aspects of services that people value or did not value have been described. Key findings are as follows:

- Overall levels of satisfaction with birth relative support services were very high, with almost three-quarters (73%) of those who had used them being almost entirely positive about the experience. Only a very small minority (6%) of birth relatives were primarily negative about their service provision. About one in five people (21%) had mixed feelings, being neither satisfied nor dissatisfied overall.
- Birth relatives valued a relationship-based service where they felt cared about and understood by a worker who empathised with their feelings and who did not judge them. It seemed important that support workers had experience and understanding of adoption issues, both because this helped the service user to feel understood and because such workers could explain the often confusing system and processes of adoption.
- Confidence in the confidentiality and independence of support services was a vital determinant of service user satisfaction.
- The needs, situations and preferences of birth relatives appeared many and varied, and therefore it seemed important that agencies provided a service that was flexible in terms of what, when and how services were offered. In many cases, birth relatives seemed to both need and value a "casework"-type service in which the worker could respond to a range of needs, both practical and emotional, and where he or she was available outside of scheduled sessions and beyond the office environment.

9 Birth relatives who had not used an adoption support service

One-third of birth relatives in the sample (n = 25, 34%) had not used any birth relative support services. Of these, some people (n = 8) were not aware of the existence of these support services. The other 17 people knew about them but had not used them. In our earlier survey of agencies, the issue of service take-up was identified as one of the key challenges in providing services to birth relatives, and why this might be the case was explored from the perspective of professionals. In this chapter, we hear directly from birth relatives about the reasons why they did not use any support services.

Did people who were not using services have unmet needs?

It is possible that some birth relatives may find the support they need from friends, family or professionals outside of the birth relative support arena. However, in our sample of birth relatives who were not using services, this rarely seemed to be the case. Only four of the 24 people (17%) who were not receiving help from a birth relative support service felt they were getting sufficient support from other sources. A birth grandmother felt she had good, regular support from the local authority social worker whenever she initiated it. Another grandmother had regular face-to-face contact with the adoptive parents of her grandchild and felt she had all the information and support she needed from them. Two birth mothers were receiving regular one-to-one support from a project helping people with learning difficulties to deal with everyday life events.

Out of the eight people who said that they were not aware that there was an independent adoption support service that could help them, six of these clearly had support needs. For example, one birth mother had her first contact letter returned to her after spending two weeks trying to write it and said she would particularly appreciate support in this area. She was also hoping for counselling. A birth father had asked his local authority for help and had not heard back from them at the time of interview. Another birth father told us that he saw a social worker from the substance misuse team every week but this was not meeting his needs: 'I do talk to them but it doesn't really help me, my problems are really deep inset now'. He said he had not been offered counselling or other support in relation to his child's adoption, but said he would take this up if it were offered. He would have liked someone to talk to regularly about his feelings and to have more reassurance about how his child was getting on. He found the chance to talk during the research interview beneficial, almost as if he saw us as a support service: '[This interview] has been the best conversation I have had this year . . . it helps to talk to people that are with it . . . it has it has been lovely . . . you are invaluable, you really are . . . it does help to have someone like yourself to talk to.'

Of the eight people who were not aware of support services, five were birth fathers or grandparents. These numbers are too small to draw any firm conclusions, but this does echo the findings in our service take-up survey that support services were more routinely offered to birth mothers whilst the needs of birth fathers and grandparents may have been overlooked.

Why do birth relatives who are aware of services not use them?

Fifteen birth relatives had received information from, had heard about, or even had an introductory meeting with, an adoption support service but had not taken up the service despite having support needs (two people said their needs were met). One birth mother said she was told that the service could not offer her help until a decision had been made regarding the child she was now pregnant with. She expressed feeling snubbed by this, 'Well, if you can't support me through the fact that she might be going, then I'm not going to bother ringing back'. She wanted help through the process and needed to talk then, not after her baby's case was over. 'You need to talk during the court case, not after, when you just want to get on with things'. However, this birth mother was the only person who said she had actually been refused a service; in other cases, there were a number of reasons why services had not been used, and these are discussed below.

Problems with reaching the venue

In three cases, despite multiple support needs, the birth relative felt unable to travel to the venue where support was to take place. One birth mother commented:

> *I got offered it but never took it up . . . I had to visit them, they don't come to you . . . I don't think they understand that my illness stops me from going out . . .*

Feeling that the service could do little to help

Some birth relatives could not see how support services could do anything to help them, key reasons being that the service was offered too early, too late or that the wrong type of service was presented. In some cases, where the adoption had not been finalised, birth relatives were focused on the fight to get their child back. They did not want "counselling" or support to cope with the adoption; in their mind, it was not going to happen. They seemed unaware that they might have been able to obtain other help like advice and information or liaison with children's services. One birth mother who declined what she described as 'counselling' said, 'Maybe because I don't want to accept, they are going to be adopted . . . I am getting them back, no matter what it takes me, I am getting them back.' A perception that counselling was all that was on offer put other people off for different reasons. A birth parent couple were clear they did not want counselling as they felt that they had not done anything wrong and it would feel like having their 'wrist slapped'. They also felt 'sick' of talking to anyone in authority. A birth father was offered 'a counselling service where if I needed to talk I could talk to her and that . . . but no, that ain't for me . . . [Counsellors would] just get into all my problems.' A couple of people felt they were not ready for counselling as the adoption was too fresh, or they were still fighting for a younger child. One grandmother had one introductory meeting with an agency but decided not to pursue it as she felt they could not do anything to change things. She also worried that the service might still have connections to children's services, with whom she had a very poor relationship.

Some birth relatives who knew the adoption of their children was finalised saw the support service as useless – the worst had happened, their child was gone, and no one could help them get them back. For example, one birth father said that whilst he would have liked help at an earlier stage, '[The worker] came in too late now because nothing nobody can do is going to help me get my kids back'.

Depression and passivity

In several cases, what seemed to stand in the way of birth relatives following up offers of help was their own sense of depression, helplessness, passivity or the need to block things out. For example, one depressed mother recalled one brief introductory meeting with an independent adoption support service some time ago and commented:

> *I wouldn't say no to meeting her again, I just don't know why I would be meeting her again . . . well, what are they going to do? . . . Nothing they can do is going to help me . . . I would like to be able to write a letter . . . I know I can ring them and say that I want to write a letter, but like I say, on a day-to-day basis I try not to think about it . . . if I thought about it all the time I would go mental . . . I could ring, it is just . . . it is just doing it . . . I am not sure [if it would help], I don't know, I don't know.*

In another case, a birth father had apparently not heard about independent adoption support until he called us offering to be interviewed. He desperately wanted someone to talk to about how things had turned out with his daughter: 'There's nobody there to talk about it. There's nobody to say "Well, you did do really well, she's doing really well now and she is happy and that".' We referred him for help and at the time of his first interview he said a support worker had called him and set a date for a meeting. However, he was unsure of when this would be and he could not remember whether he was going to go and see them or whether they were coming to him. He admitted that because of all the 'fighting' to get his daughter back, he was 'very forgetful . . . I've got that much going through me mind at the moment that it's hard to concentrate on anything'. He asked us to give him the support agency's number again so that he could call and check. At the time of his second interview he remembered seeing the support worker just once but he was very unclear about what came out of this, explaining that he was still depressed at the time. He could not remember whether he was supposed to call them for another appointment or whether they were supposed to call him.

Another birth mother, whom we referred for help after her first interview, told us over a year later that she had not had any contact from the support agency. She then admitted they might have written but explained that she often does not open mail during low periods in her life: 'I might have been sick and just ignored the letter or whatever'. She asked us to inform them again that she would like them to get in touch, saying, 'They should not give up on me like when I am upset and don't want to talk, I don't want them to give up on me'.

Lack of follow-up from the agency

As the experience of the birth mother in the paragraph above indicates, there may be a need in many cases for agencies to pursue initial enquiries quite vigorously. In several cases this did not seem to have happened (although, as the birth mother above suggested, it is possible that people did not remember or take in further contacts). Three birth relatives who had had some brief contact, such as an introductory session with an independent adoption support service, were still waiting to receive the support they hoped for. In all cases, there seemed to be a lack of clarity as to whether the agency was expected to call them for further appointments or whether the birth relative themselves was to make the next move. In these cases, birth relatives generally seemed to take a passive approach and wait for others to contact them rather than make the move themselves, despite sometimes being very needy. For example, a grandmother said during her first interview that she would like 'Just somebody to talk to really, because I spend most of my time looking after [my daughter] and supporting [my daughter]. And basically I don't have any time for myself.' By her second interview, she had phoned the support service but was still waiting for someone to come out: 'They were going to come out and see me but they never got round to it'.

Summary

This chapter has described the experiences of birth relatives who have not used any adoption support services. Key findings are as follows:

- One-third of birth relatives in our sample had not used adoption support services, and most of these had unmet needs.
- Some people had no recollection of being offered a service and had no awareness of what might be available. But in more cases people did know services were there, but a number of factors prevented them from accessing services.
- Four factors relating to why birth relatives had not used services were identified. These were: problems reaching the venue; feeling that the service could not meet their needs; feelings of depression and passivity; and the lack of active follow-up from the agency.

10 Other sources of support for birth relatives

Birth relatives were asked about other sources of support for the adoption, formal and informal, which they had received, and this chapter describes these.

Mental health services

Mental ill health in birth relatives could both precede and be exacerbated by the child's adoption. Some people were already engaged with mental health services prior to the adoption; however, consistent provision which continued through the process and beyond was rarely described. In the interview, people described receiving services from a range of health professionals, including general practitioners (5 people); counsellors (19 people); psychotherapists, psychologists or psychiatrists (6 people) and community psychiatric nurses (3 people).

The majority of birth relatives talked in mainly negative terms about the talking-based therapies provided by mental health professionals. As we have already seen, some people seemed to find the prospect or experience of counselling difficult, and the most common reasons given for not liking counselling were that it was too painful or difficult to talk about their feelings or their past, and/or that it could not achieve anything. Some people felt that the counsellor had their own agenda to cover, or fixed ideas about the cause of the problem. Most counselling did not focus specifically on adoption, and some people even felt the professional discouraged a focus on adoption. In some cases it seemed that the birth relatives themselves did not bring the topic up. For example, one birth mother, who approached her GP for help, commented:

I haven't actually told my doctor why I am depressed. I just said I was depressed and that I could do with being put on some medication, I didn't go into any details with the doctor really . . . I just didn't want to talk about it.

One birth mother (who was parenting her youngest child) raised the issue of trust, feeling that she could not have complete confidence in her psychotherapist knowing that information could be passed on to others:

> *He is mental health, they have to, it goes in my file . . . and that pisses me off, because as far as I am concerned psychotherapy or counselling should be confidential.*

Four birth relatives did express positive experiences of mental health services and they all seemed to be people who were open to thinking and talking about difficult feelings and experiences. For example, one birth mother explained how a psychologist had done some 'really deep work' into her past:

> *They really go back to see where the trouble actually started, and it was quite an eye opener really, and you start to realise yourself where it started and how far back it goes . . . It has opened my eyes a lot.*

Foster carers

Foster carers of the birth relatives' children were mentioned by eight people as being understanding and helpful throughout, and sometimes beyond, the time when the children were placed with them. Most of these birth relatives said that they would have liked their child to stay with and be adopted by the foster carer if the child was not able to come home (in one case this occurred and regular face-to-face contact continued between them). The foster carers were appreciated for passing on information that they were unable to get from children's services and for including them in their child's achievements: 'She has always given me school photos, every time she has took them away she has brought photos back and she has never stopped me from phoning them on things like birthdays'. One birth mother, who had a very good relationship with the foster carer who had looked after her children for two years, very much wanted to stay in touch with her, but children's services had apparently told her that she was not able to. She found this very hurtful and planned to go and see the foster carer when released from prison: 'I have never forgot about her and when I get out they can't stop me from going to see her'.

Family, partners and friends

When asked who else they felt they could turn to for support regarding the adoption, although most people did mention at least one person who was a partner, family member or friend, problems with getting support from these people were reported by half of birth relatives: 17 people (23%) either did not identify any friends or family or specifically said that they felt they had no one who had supported them. A further 20 people (27%) mentioned specific issues they had experienced in relation to getting support from friends and family.

Some birth parents had stayed with their partner after the adoption of their children. In some cases, people felt that they and their partner had been able to help and support each other, or even that the adoption had brought them closer together. But in many more cases, birth parents had split up either before or after the adoption and in several of these situations one parent blamed the other for the adoption; they were estranged and could not support each other. For some birth parents (in both intact and separated couples), although people were not hostile to each other, it was hard for them to support each other. A particular issue here involved birth parents dealing with the adoption in different ways, for example, one person wanting to talk about the adoption but the other preferring to avoid the subject. Some people in new relationships felt they could not mention the adoption to their new partner. In one case, a birth mother said she was afraid to mention that she had lost a child to adoption in case it put off any potential new partner. Some birth parents said that their new partner had needs of their own, and so they did not want to impose their worries onto them.

Many birth relatives experienced problems within their family. In some cases, people's relationships with their family had broken down before the adoption happened, with many people reporting being abused, neglected or rejected by their family. Other people felt that the adoption had caused family splits, for example, one paternal grandmother said that, as a result of the adoption, her partner had left her and she was on bad terms with her son. Some birth relatives, often grandparents, were so involved in caring for another birth relative that their own needs remained unmet. For example, one grandmother told us how the birth mother would ring her up almost every night in tears. She was pleased to be able to support her but at the same time found this both depressing and draining, adding to her own burden. Another grandmother said that her daughter (the birth mother) 'never stopped crying . . . I was the one who had to pick the pieces up . . . I didn't get a chance to grieve at all.' Several people referred to adoption as being a taboo topic within their family. The fear of causing upset could mean reluctance to raise the topic, and feelings related to the adoption could also include shame, guilt, regret and anger against family members for causing or contributing to the loss of the child. For example, one birth father explained:

> *I don't talk about it to anybody because (pause) it's not an everyday conversation, is it . . . my mother, she won't mention it much 'cos she knows that it might upset me or she don't know what to say. She feels guilty . . . no one says anything . . . It's like, it's (pause) no man's land, what everyone's learnt to avoid.*

One young birth mother living at home with her parents and suffering from depression spoke of how her daughter (and their granddaughter) was never referred to in the home:

> *Since I have been to court and they know she is not coming back, the honest truth is that they have never said anything about it, they haven't said a thing, not a word to me about it . . . I think they probably feel guilty. They are probably scared to talk to me about it because they know that they could have helped me.*

Another birth mother felt unable to raise the topic of the adoption with her mother, partly because she felt ashamed of being unable to parent her sons, but also because her mother did not apply to look after the boys. Despite rationally understanding why her mother could not adopt them herself, she struggled with this fact: 'If I think about them not going for my kids, I will hate them and I don't want to hate them'.

In terms of getting support from friends and others outside of the family, people's experiences were mixed. In one extreme case, a birth mother told us that she had to move to a completely different area because of abuse from her neighbours when her children were taken away. More commonly, people talked about the difficulties they felt in talking about the adoption to others, the negative reactions of others, or the difficulties that other people seemed to have in knowing how to react. For example, one birth father talked about his problems with other people, and about how the way he had reacted to the crisis of the adoption had isolated him from support when he needed it most:

> *[The fact that my child has been adopted] has caused problems with some people . . . They look at you like you have crapped in their hand-bag or something and you get that a lot . . . People just treat you like scum . . . they just make assumptions . . . I don't really have many friends to tell you the truth. Our [Rob] . . . has been my best mate for years . . . he says, 'At least you have got kids and you know they are there somewhere,' but that is not enough and so you can't really mention it . . . One of my mates did tell me that people don't know how to react around me . . . I was in a pretty bad way for a few months and a lot of people gave me a wide berth because I was a bit frighten-ing . . . I try not to mention [the adoption] these days . . . they don't want to hear it.*

Support from local authority children's services

Although many birth relatives had very angry and hostile feelings towards professionals working in children's services, the most common "other" source of support identified by birth relatives was from children's services, particularly from post adoption teams and workers supporting indirect contact.

Many birth relatives had had dealings with the local authority letter-box contact support service and people's experiences of this varied widely. From some parents' perspectives, contact teams were seen as primarily having an administrative and censuring role to ensure "appropriate" letters were exchanged (this is something birth relatives also reported in relation to direct contact in our parallel study (Neil *et al*, 2010). Many people said they had only received contact information indirectly, such as in the form of a letter outlining the "rules" of contact.

Information or help regarding contact might only have been given once and subsequently been forgotten; one birth mother remembered getting advice about writing contact letters but could not take it in 'because I was full of hate of social services at the time'. One birth parent said that the contact worker had spoken to her 'like I was a little child'. Those people who experienced the letterbox service as a censoring system could be reluctant or afraid to ask for help in dealing with contact issues in case their contact was stopped. Letters which took a great deal of time to write but were returned led to particularly bad feelings.

Other people reported much more positive experiences, and at least 11 people were particularly positive about their contact workers: 'She is fab . . . she is really approachable, she is really easy to contact, and if I ever have any questions about something I am not quite sure about, I give her a ring'. Another birth mother praised her worker for always phoning up immediately if there was anything wrong with her letters and dealing with problems in a constructive and positive way: 'It was all positive feedback, it was just suggesting I should alter this slightly or maybe say this instead of that, and that was fine . . . She speaks to me like I am a human being, more than that, she speaks to me like I am a mother . . . I still gave birth to them and she respects that.' Some people had been encouraged to call the contact team or worker and had received help or support via letter, over the phone, or in person. Problems with contact could be discussed and advice received, for example, one birth father, keen to receive more photos of his child, was advised to write to the adoptive parents to ask for this. There were also examples of contact teams/workers providing more proactive support (offering help or providing a courtesy call at home even when not requested) or acting on the behalf of birth relatives to ensure that adoptive parents kept up contact. One birth mother referred to the contact worker as supportive and 'on her side' and said that the contact worker was 'disgusted' with the adoptive parents' attitude towards her. Workers who came out to the birth relative's home to help with letters or life story work were nearly always appreciated, and it seemed that these local authority workers could undertake the same type of work that other people received from independent support workers:

The lady there sat with us and she went through the letter, she gave me a draft and she gave ideas. She drafted the letter for me and I sat afterwards and copied it out . . . I got upset and that and she asked me if I wanted a little bit of time on my own . . . which was nice . . . I found them very helpful and again not judgemental and quite understanding really and they showed sympathy . . . They sat down with me and they didn't try and tell me what to write, they just gave me a guideline and let me get it into my head.

Some people referred to receiving help or advice from their post-adoption or contact team that was not necessarily contact-related. A regular or occasional opportunity to speak with an empathic worker who knew the case and could understand their situation was seen as comforting in a few cases. In some cases, in-house workers were a useful link to independent adoption support services; for example, one letterbox co-ordinator refer-red a birth father to the support service and phoned up on his behalf to arrange the first appointment. The continued connection that such depart-ments had with birth relatives over a long period of time meant that referrals could be made at appropriate times, picking up birth relatives who may have refused services offered at an earlier stage.

As with all interactions with professionals, there were some negative experiences, such as issues with the availability of staff. One birth mother claimed that every time she had tried to ring for help with her letter writing, no-one had been there, 'so I thought, sod this, I'll do it myself . . . they're always busy or in a meeting, or they're on sick leave'. Some birth relatives felt they could not relate positively to individual workers. Some saw the letterbox service's connection to the agency which had been involved with the removal of their child as an issue: 'I don't like going in . . . what has happened to me I just don't trust social services, I would never ever trust them again.'

Advocacy services

Access to an advocacy service appeared to be an unusual experience for birth relatives in the study. Only one person referred to having had the involvement of an independent advocate (in this case a disability advocate) at the time of the court case, arranged by social services. This birth mother's partner (who was present during her interview and who added his own comments) explained the role of the disability advocate:

She used to come to the house and talk to [my partner] to try and comfort her and all that . . . She used to explain to her what the courts were for and what they were going to do . . . [my partner] couldn't understand with the learning difficulties and she used to try and put it into a simpler form for her so she could understand.

Other sources of support

Other services which birth relatives mentioned as good sources of support included a local volunteer bureau, a family centre, a local charity providing a range of day-care opportunities and support services for people with learning disabilities, a local Connexions service and churches. It was clear that occasionally people were able to tap into excellent support, which, although not adoption-specific, was able to help in a very empathic and accommodating manner, targeting adoption-related needs for information, practical help and emotional support – working in a similar way to independent adoption support services. For example, one birth mother had recently discovered that the support worker from her local charity provision for people with learning difficulties was a birth mother too, and 'she understands what I'm going through'. The independence of these services from social services was appreciated. One birth mother, who was extremely positive about the help and support she had recently been getting from her local Connexions service, had been very dissatisfied with help from her independent adoption support worker (whom she had not viewed as truly independent). The Connexions worker seemed to provide a distance from the local authority provision, which (along with the worker's open approach) led to increased trust:

It was not her line of work but she said she didn't care and to tell her what was wrong, and that was when she made an appointment to come out and see me . . . She was able to sit there and just listen to what I had to say. I can't get that from social services; they never offered me no support when I went through bad times with kids whatsoever . . . She comes to see me and she asks how things are and how things are going and if I have got any support . . . and even tries to find things out on my behalf . . . Everything I say to her, unless there is concern, is confidential and she has kept her word . . . I really do get on well with her.

Three people had received a range of valued help from local church communities, including the provision of an independent venue for contact whilst a child was in foster care and a pastor offering support every day on the phone. One birth mother commented that her church had provided her with more support than anywhere else. She had been able to talk about the adoption and link up with someone in the congregation who worked for Sure Start and who could give her parenting ideas to help her with another child who was at home. She found her church was always a source of people to speak to and experienced a boost to her self-esteem when someone had let her hold their new baby: 'It made me feel like I wasn't as useless as they think I am'.

Summary

This chapter has looked at what other help was available for birth relatives in dealing with the problems that followed the loss of a child to adoption. Key findings are as follows:

- Despite the fact that many birth relatives have mental health issues, only a minority of people mentioned receiving regular specialist NHS mental health services (other than GP visits or the prescription of medication). Most people who had used talking-based therapies did not find these useful in dealing with issues related to the adoption.
- A few birth relatives felt they had received valuable support from the foster carers of the children.
- The majority of birth relatives mentioned using friends or family for support. However, about a quarter of people (23%) felt they had "no one" who had supported them. Over a quarter of people (27%) described problems that prevented them from getting support from friends and family.

- The most common source of other support mentioned by birth relatives was local authority children's services, in particular, letterbox support workers, and post-adoption team workers.
- Other sources of support included volunteer bureaux, family centres, learning disability services, Connexions, and churches.

11 Coping with adoption

Chapter 6 explored birth relatives' accounts of their feelings about the child's adoption at the time it took place. This chapter focuses on how birth relatives were feeling at the time that we interviewed them, looking specifically at how people were "living with", "adjusting to" or "coping with" the losses, challenges and changes that adoption had brought about. Our aims here were to explore and attempt to measure aspects of adjustment that are relevant to birth relatives' own welfare, and (given that almost all adoptions involve some form of contact with the adopted child) aspects of adjustment that are likely to be relevant to the child's welfare.

Developing a measurement of "coping with adoption"

To attempt to understand and measure differences in how birth relatives cope with the challenges of adoption immediately begs questions about what is a "good" outcome. Because the majority of people in our sample had long-standing difficulties that predated the adoption, we rejected the idea that a "good" outcome could be measured only by positive indicators of people's broad psychosocial functioning. We also knew from previous work with birth parents in adoption, and the bereavement literature generally, that "good" outcomes were unlikely to mean a cessation of negative emotion or disconnection from thoughts and feelings about the child: the notion of "getting over" the experience was inappropriate. Neither did the term "accepting" adoption seem entirely right, as many people we had spoken to (both interviewees and people in our birth relative consultant groups) rejected this term, arguing that, when the adoption had been forced against the birth parents' wishes, the notion that he or she should "accept" this was inappropriate. Previous qualitative analysis of a similar sample of contemporary birth relatives identified three different patterns of feelings about the adoption seven years after the event: positive acceptance; resignation; anger and resistance (Neil, 2007a). We considered using these categories, but in the current sample of people much closer to the event, clear patterns did not seem to have

147

emerged in many cases. We therefore decided to start our analysis afresh with the current sample, working through a number of stages summarised below.

1) *Exploring the meaning of "coping with adoption" with our reference groups of birth relatives.* Briefly, this involved selecting four interviews felt by the research team to represent a range of ways of dealing with adoption. These interviews were edited to form four 10-minute "scripts" which were then read by actors and recorded. These recordings were then played to our two groups of birth relatives and people were asked to assess how well each person was coping with adoption (assigning a number from 1–10) and give reasons for their answers. We asked people to consider aspects of coping with adoption that were positive for the birth relative themselves and aspects of dealing with the experience that were likely to be "good" for the adopted child. Key messages about understanding the notion of "coping with" adoption were then summarised at the end of this process and taken forward for consideration at the next stage.

2) *Using feedback from the birth relative reference groups, insights from previous research and consideration of our own data, the research team identified three dimensions of dealing with adoption*: managing dual connection, feelings about the outcomes of adoption for the child and dealing with the impact of adoption on self. Descriptions of each of these were drafted and, on a sample of five interview transcripts, each coder independently rated cases as high, medium or low, giving reasons. Using feedback from this, definitions were then refined and it was decided to use a five point scale for the first dimension and three points for the other two dimensions. Descriptions and examples of each point on the scale were written into the coding handbook as more cases were examined.

3) *Applying this rating scale to all cases by members of the coding team, using the coding handbook, with any difficult decisions being referred to another coder for discussion.* Cases were coded using the case summary for each case, plus an examination of the relevant nodes in Nvivo. All interviews (Time 1 and Time 2) were coded so we could

look at changes over time. All coding was then checked by one coder (the director of the study) to ensure consistency of coding.

Accepting dual connection

An adopted child is a member of two families. This creates certain challenges for him or her: to establish a coherent sense of identity, to make sense of where they belong, to understand the different roles of their two sets of parents, and to be aware of why they were adopted. The child's adoption also challenges birth relatives to negotiate a major psychosocial transition, events described by Parkes as those which give rise to 'major changes in life space which are lasting in their effects, which take place over a relatively short period of time and which affect large areas of the assumptive world' (1971, p 103). Birth relatives must understand their change in role from being the legal relative to having no legal relationship with the child; from being or expecting to be a psychological parent to having someone else take over this role; from being the child's only mum or dad to understanding that another person is to be known by this name; to work out what being a "birth" parent or grandparent actually means. Just as the child has to make sense of their identity, these issues also challenge birth relatives to think about: 'Who and what am I to my child now?' and perhaps to answer these questions from other people in their social world. Brodzinsky (2005) argues that it is healthiest for the child if both adoptive parents and birth parents can recognise and support the child's membership of both families. Given that most adoptions now include some form of openness, the extent to which birth relatives can accept the child's membership of the adoptive family is relevant to the child's welfare after they are adopted.

This dimension was rated on a five-point scale, 5 being high (almost all positive indicators applied) and 1 being low (almost no positive indicators applied). A score of 4 was allocated for cases with more positives than negatives, 3 where there was no clear predominance of positive or negatives, and 2 for cases with more negatives than positives. In rating this dimension, we drew heavily on what birth relatives thought about the child's place in the adoptive family. Consequently, the scale was only applied in cases where the adoptive placement had at least been identified.

Positive indicators

Birth parents and grandparents who scored highly on this dimension made statements and comments which showed that they recognised, accepted, valued, supported and promoted the child's membership of both families, as opposed to claiming an exclusive role as the real family. The vast majority of birth relatives told us they still felt their own connection to the child very strongly, and believed that this would persist over time, and this was not seen as negative indicator. However, some birth relatives were more able than others to recognise that their family was not the child's only family. One birth mother explained this complex phenomenon as follows:

> In some ways I feel they are still mine and they will always be mine. But in another I feel they are not mine totally any more, because they are not with me any more and they are there . . . they are mine in my heart but they are not in person, do you know what I mean? I have got to think to myself – well, I have to give them up partly.

Birth relatives who scored highly on this dimension recognised that they no longer had any status as the child's legal relative, and that this change was permanent, for example, by recognising that reclaiming the child was not possible; by realising that it is up to the child whether they seek them out in the future and what type of relationship they will have with them; and by understanding that contact would be limited and that in decisions about contact, the adoptive parents' and child's wishes were dominant. For example, a grandmother said that contact arrangements 'should be [adoptive mum's] decisions . . . because she is looking after the children now'. They recognised the child's need to settle, be loved, and feel secure in the new family. One birth mother said the following about her children, who had very recently been placed for adoption:

> I hope that [the children] do bond with them as far as that is possible and develop a positive relationship with their adopters. And I hope that each, the adopters and [the children], can accept the new roles that they are now in . . . I hope the family relationship does emerge and develop. That's what I wish for [the children].

Some birth relatives showed awareness of the child's potential feelings, thoughts and questions (depending on their age and the nature of previous relationships) about their birth family. For example, one birth mother whose children were old enough to remember having lived with her, said her motivation for writing to her children was 'so they could see that I haven't forgot them and I am happy for them and that and they can see I am doing fine'. Feelings of hurt and pain over the loss of role with the child, or feelings of discomfort about adoptive parents taking over the legal and psychological parenting of the child, were common and not seen as contraindicators, providing the birth relative was able to put these feelings aside and not allow them to dominate their thoughts and actions. One birth mother talked about how sad she was that the adoptive parents had taken over her role, and the title of "mummy", but she understood why this was necessary and did what was asked of her when replying to letters:

I should be doing all those things with them, but someone else is doing it . . . It hurts me a little bit because [the adoptive parents] didn't put "mummy" [on the letter] . . . it hurts me but I understand that they have to call [the adoptive parents] mum and dad.

In some cases, birth relatives were able to take pleasure in the thought of their child loving, and being loved by, their new parents. Some birth parents and grandparents talked explicitly about the possible complications for the child of having two families, and the subsequent need for both sets of parents to work together. The following birth mother expressed this perfectly:

I think it will be important that the child knows that the parents can work together, that the birth and the adoptive parents can work together. I think it would be very helpful for them to know they're not going to be torn or feel like they're being deceitful to their adoptive parents who've brought them up most of their life.

In rating acceptance of dual connection, we took account not just of how birth relatives said they felt, but of how they described they had behaved in relevant situations, for instance, in any contact they had had with adoptive parents. Parents and grandparents who scored highly on this dimension were those who told us they accepted and worked within reasonable boundaries and limitations of contact (but may have taken steps to make changes if contact was not working). For example, one grandmother of five siblings (the oldest three lived with her and the youngest two were adopted) explained how she talked to the older children about the need not to ask their younger brothers questions about where they lived. She explained to them, 'They have got to be safe like you are safe'. Positive indicators also included showing an understanding of contact in terms of the child's needs, for example, that it may be important for the child in dealing with issues related to identity, separation and loss. Some birth relatives used contact to convey their acceptance of placement to the child and adopters, to express their positive feelings for the child, and to pass on relevant family or medical information. They showed willingness (where the opportunity allowed) to meet adoptive parents, to contribute to life story work, and to persist with contact even when difficulties occurred.

Negative indicators

Some people had unrealistic expectations about the child having an ongoing bond with them that was higher in quality than – and never to be replaced by – their bond with the adoptive parents. A few people admitted to the desire to actively reclaim the child, seeing this as their right and feeling that the child was "theirs", without recognising the impact it could have on a child to be moved from a settled family placement. For example, the following birth mother's child had been taken away five years ago, and had been with his adoptive parents for two years. She told us:

> *I always look at kids on the street and I'd get out and bring him back, like any other parent would do . . . I don't think my son sees [the adopters] as parents, he's only got one [set of] parents . . . They are just carers looking after him, that's how I look at it . . . He doesn't want a new mummy and daddy . . . [He] will not call them mummy and daddy because it's not his mummy and daddy.*

Feelings that the adoption should not have happened, or that the process was unfair, were widespread amongst the people we interviewed. Feelings such as these, by themselves, were not taken as evidence of an inability to accept dual connection. However, in some cases, birth relatives' feelings about the adoption being unjust had an impact on their ability to accept the reality of adoption; they maintained a position of protest and fighting for their child's return even after all hope of this was gone. For example, one birth mother whose children had been adopted over two years ago said:

> *I'll get them babies and I'm going to get justice for them . . . With my friend we are going to do leaflets and a protest and get petitions signed and everything to change the law and go to court and give us our children back and prosecute social services.*

Feelings about adoptive parents were not necessarily totally negative – birth relatives may have seen them as nice people and good carers but just not like *real parents* or a *proper family*. One birth father, who expressed no animosity towards the adoptive parents, talked about his child's need to be moved back 'into the normal birth family'. Other people expressed the view that the adoptive parents were substitute or temporary carers, acting on their behalf: 'I am still his mum; they are just looking after him for me'. Some birth relatives did not show any interest in the adoptive family; they simply refused to think about them. In some cases, the parent or grandparent had unrealistic hopes for the future. For example, one birth mother said, 'When the children are 18 or whatever, they will come back and they are going to hate that woman [the adoptive mother] and they are not even going to thank her'.

In a small number of cases, birth relatives downplayed or denied the child's connection to the birth family, instead having a rejecting attitude or not showing any understanding that the child might need to maintain a connection, or that the birth family might be important to them. For example, one birth mother said that she had never felt a connection to one of her children:

> *Because I just didn't want him from day one . . . if he comes [to see me when he was older] I would give him a cup of coffee and I would say*

'bye'. If [he] had to have a liver transplant or something like that, I would say, 'You need not look at me'.

In terms of actions described, indicators of lack of acceptance of dual connection included resisting attempts to take part in contact, for instance, refusing to meet adoptive parents or write letters. For example, one birth father explained that he had been told he could write to the children but that he had to sign his name rather than "dad". He would not agree to this: 'cos it hurts too much'. He did not want to write to the adoptive parents, only directly to the children. His difficulty in accepting that someone else would be taking over his role was apparent in his explanation of why he refused to meet the adoptive parents:

You've got to sit there, listening to these daft bastards waffle on about what they do for your kid when you are the father of the bairn and you can do the stuff that he's been babbling about and you're not allowed to do it.

In other cases, birth relatives maintained contact in an unhelpful way, for example, by being unable to contain their own feelings of anger or loss.

Feelings about the outcomes of adoption for the child

In a previous examination of birth relatives' feelings about adoption by Neil (2007a), how people felt about the outcome of the adoption for the child emerged as an important theme. Feeling confident that the child was happy and loved in the adoptive family seemed a very important part of managing the difficult feelings that often surrounded the adoption. A hope or confidence that the child was having a good life appeared to mitigate some of the pain of adoption both for parents who had relinquished their children and for those whose children were adopted from care; some parents expressed this in words such as 'something good has come out of something bad'. A feeling that things had worked out for the child seemed related to people's ability to move on in other areas – in some cases, to let go of anger, blame or guilt. A sense of assurance about the child's welfare seemed to be both an indicator of positive aspects of adjustment for the birth relative and a predictor of other positive outcomes, for example, accepting dual connection.

In the current study, we rated people's feelings about the outcomes of adoption for the child on a three-point scale: positive (there was a clear predominance of positive indicators applying – score 5); mixed (there was no clear predominance of positive or negatives – score 3) and negative (there was a clear predominance of negative indicators applying – score 1).

In examining how birth relatives felt the adoption was working out for their child, all birth relatives referred to the information they had or did not have to inform this opinion. Many people referred to the positive impact of having met the adoptive parents or having contact after adoption. Without having met the adoptive parents, and without any contact, it seemed very difficult for birth relatives to be confident that their child was OK. As one birth mother put it:

> *Getting contact was a turning point . . . [without contact] you just worry yourself. I can't understand how any mother . . . could possibly move on with their life without knowing [her children] were alright.*

Anxieties about the adopted child were common. In some cases, people expressed a general sense of anxiety that they argued was "normal" for parents or grandparents to feel, and that they did not expect to ever go away. For example, one mother who generally felt confident that her son was OK said, 'You can't help having that bit in your mind that he is unhappy, or he could be unhappy. I don't think for a minute he is, but I can't help having that little bit of doubt.' Where birth parents spoke about this type of worry, but otherwise were positive about the outcomes of adoption for the child, we coded them as "positive" overall. Quite a few birth relatives claimed to have absolutely no current information about the child. Often these were people experiencing the "contact gap" – they had said goodbye to their child but post-adoption contact had not started. Some people who had no or very little information had all kinds of worries about their child, even wondering if they were being abused or if they were alive or dead, and these people were coded as being "negative" overall. Other people who actually knew very little about their child, nevertheless tried to take an optimistic view; for instance, one mother in this position said, 'You have got to think that your kid is alright . . . you want your child to have a good life – I hope she is.' When people like this birth mother had no specific anxieties, we coded them as "mixed".

The positive and negative indicators of this dimension are illustrated below.

Positive indicators

- Comments which showed that the birth relative had peace of mind that their child was OK, e.g. 'I feel better in a way because I know [my daughter] is going to be well looked after'.
- Feelings of reassurance that the child was being cared for properly and loved by the adopters, that the adopters were good parents, e.g. 'I know my children are being looked after and being cared for and being loved'; 'They are making her happy'.
- Expressions of trust in the adoptive parents' parenting decisions; feeling confident they would do the best for the child and not let them come to harm, emotionally and physically. 'The black woman's going to look after [my daughter] because she'll know how to look after her skin and hair and stuff'.
- Feeling positive about the child's developmental progress. e.g. 'They are growing up so well'.
- Feeling positive about the educational, financial and leisure opportunities available to the child, and possibly feeling that the child is now better off than in the birth family, e.g. 'They are having lots of opportunities . . . I probably wouldn't have been able to give them as much as the adopters. I know it is not all about material things like holidays, but it all sounds sort of happy and sunny'; 'It has all worked out for the best'.
- General feelings of optimism about adoption, such as assuming that an adopted child must be very much wanted and that adoptive parents have been assessed as being suitable, and that help is available if needed, e.g. 'Adoption is a lot better now and there is a lot more support out there for children as well as the parents'.

Negative indicators

- Having no confidence that all was well for the child, e.g. 'I don't even know if she is still alive'.
- Specific worries about the child's health, development or happiness, e.g. 'I worry about [his] eating problems'.
- Worries about aspects of how the child was being parented, e.g. 'They are making them go to Sunday school every weekend and I don't agree with that – to me weekends are the time you spend with your kids'.
- Feeling unhappy about particular characteristics of the adoptive parents, e.g. their ethnicity or sexual orientation, 'It's going to be hard for [my son] because he's been put with two women. It scares me – that fact that when he is older he is going to get bullied'.
- Fears that the child may be abused, e.g. 'I was in foster care when I was younger and it was horrible, so every time I am thinking about them I am thinking "Is this woman hitting my children, or is she beating them?" '
- Negativity or anxiety around lack of information about their child's life and/or the adoptive parents, e.g. 'I don't know anything. It's just a constant stress'.
- A lack of confidence in the adoption system generally, e.g. 'They said that they assessed them and all that but . . . I got no trust at all'.
- Feeling the child was unhappy about being adopted and wanted to come "home", e.g. 'I feel as though I am doing a [prison] sentence . . . and it's not just on my side – the children must feel the same'.
- Worries that the adoptive parents would not meet their child's specific needs e.g. 'I worry that if he does have special needs and they decide they can't cope with it, will they keep him or not?'

Dealing with the impact of adoption on self

As we have seen in earlier sections, and in the literature review, having a child or grandchild adopted almost always precipitates negative emotions for the parent or grandparents, including a sense of loss and bereavement, feelings of guilt, shame or stigma and anger. For some people these negative emotions bring about deterioration in the ability to function at their usual level socially and psychologically. Our birth relative consultants drew our attention particularly to the need to consider how well birth relatives cope with managing negative emotional states, including feelings about themselves and the practical and social challenges of trying to carry on with life after such a difficult experience. Thus we attempted to examine and measure how well the birth parent/ relative was dealing with the impact of the adoption on their lives. Key areas we considered were:

- how people think about themselves in relation to the adoption;
- dealing with negative emotions;
- getting on with life;
- the ability to take positive actions to help themselves.

We rated "dealing with the impact of adoption on self" on a three-point scale: positive (there was a clear predominance of positive indicators applying – score 5); mixed (where there was no clear predominance of positive or negatives – score 3); negative (there was a clear predominance of negative indicators applying – score 1). The positive and negative indicators that we used in our coding are outlined in more detail below.

Positive indicators

Parents and grandparents who scored highly on this dimension were those who showed evidence that they could think largely non-defensively about the reasons why the child had been adopted, avoiding extremes of either denial or guilt and shame. We use the word "extreme" here because to expect a person to be entirely without defences seemed unreasonable, but unless a parent completely denied any failing, some level of guilt seemed an inevitable consequence. For example, the following birth mother's child was removed because of her mental health issues and problems caused by her partner's drug addiction. In talking about this she said, 'Yeah, I have made mistakes, and to me I have paid for them'. She talked about her guilt saying, 'You have got the guilt and I don't care what anybody says, for any parent that has lost a child to adoption there is guilt and it is hard to live with guilt'. Despite this, she was able to say, 'I am not a bad person,' and argued, 'There is really only one person that makes you feel better and that is yourself'.

Some people managed to achieve an honest compromise – admitting their failings but avoiding low self-worth – by thinking about the reasons or circumstances behind their situation at the time. For example, the following birth mother whose children were adopted because of her drug use, domestic violence, and her mental health problems talked about how she reached a point where she 'decided that it was about time to actually give myself permission to be happy and get on with my life' and her ability to do this was partly because she was able to think that what she 'put her kids through' was not 'intentionally, but because I was unwell'. Another birth mother said, 'I didn't know how to raise my children because I hadn't been parented properly myself'.

In talking about their role as a "birth" relative after adoption, some people made statements or described actions that indicated a sense of self-worth and worth to the child, for example, by recognising that they might still have something to offer the child or adoptive parents through participating in contact or helping with life story work. The following mother related her positive sense of self to her ability to write to her children, 'I love being able to write to my children now and actually have something interesting to say'.

Another positive indicator was the determination some people showed to take positive steps to improve their situation or the situation of others. One birth mother described her desire to recover very simply: 'I want to get better'. Some parents talked about what they would need to change if they were to be successful in parenting children in the future. For example, one mother, whose child was removed primarily because of violence between her and her partner, and because of their drinking, said:

We thought that if we wanted another child in the future, then we had to change and settle down and there was no point in us stopping together if we were just going to fight and argue. I have realised that we have made mistakes . . . and if you want a good future you have got to move on from that past.

In some cases, parents talked about steps they were going to take, or were taking, to address their personal problems; for example, one mother said, 'We want to go to counselling so we can put things right, bad things we have done in the past'. Another said, 'I am working on my anger at the moment and what triggers it and how I deal with certain situations'. Others sought out support or took up offers of support to deal with their loss. One birth mother began giving talks to others about her experiences, saying, 'If I can help just one person and stop them going through what I went through, then obviously it has got to be worthwhile'. In some cases, the positive steps that people took were in relation to post-adoption contact – they were actively trying to get contact started or suggesting changes when things were not working.

More generally, an indicator of positive coping was the ability to carry on with, or re-engage with wider life activities, for instance, education, work and social life. One birth mother took pride in telling us, 'I have done some exams; I have passed City and Guilds for English and Maths . . . I have done a computer course and I passed that and I bought an old computer.' Some birth relatives explicitly referred to "getting on" with their lives. In some cases, they presented the ability to resume activities as evidence of coping. In other cases, birth relatives seemed to use engagement in activities as a means of coping. For example, one birth father said, 'I think if I keep myself busy it's not too bad . . . maybe that's why I am a bit better'. In order to able to resume a "normal" (for the individual) level of functioning, many people described an improvement in symptoms or problems that were precipitated by the loss of the child, for example, they felt less depressed, or had stopped or reduced drinking or taking drugs, or they no longer self-harmed.

All birth relatives we interviewed talked about the negative feelings associated with adoption, and so the presence or persistence of these was not seen as contraindicating positive coping. Many people said they expected feelings of loss to never go away; one mother said her grief was 'a part of me'. The child continues to exists and grow and change, and so it is not just the baby or toddler or young child that is lost, but the young child, the teenager, the emerging adult, the parent of your grandchildren. As one mother said, 'You know they are going to get older and they are going to change in little ways and be their own little people. And you want to be there every day to see them . . . and you can't'. However, some people talked about finding ways to "deal with", "live with" or "accept" negative emotions. For example, one grandparent said, 'I know what people mean now by "learning to live" with a loss. You do think about it, but you do live with it'. Some people felt the intensity of their emotions would not change, but their ability to cope with them had. For example, one birth mother said:

> *Like any grief, you go through various stages and I am very lucky to have reached the acceptance stage now. It doesn't hurt any less and I am no less angry than I was, but I have had to accept that no amount of screaming and crying and shouting is going to change the situation. All I can do now is try and make the best of my life, so that when my children come looking for me in the future, they find a well balanced woman rather than the mess they left behind.*

In other cases, birth relatives did describe a lessening intensity of negative emotions:

> *The pain is the same but it is getting easier, it is diminishing . . . it's not as raw as it was a year ago . . . I have got used to the feeling and I live with how it feels and it gradually gets easier. It is not more pleasant, it is just not as raw.*

Some birth relatives were able to identify some positive feelings associated with adoption. For example, the following birth mother said about her children, 'I can picture them . . . and it's not unpleasant . . . it's happy memories, it is like a warm happy feeling . . . so it's not unpleasant to talk about it, or to talk about them.' Some people experienced positive feelings especially on hearing news of their children, though these were often mixed with sadness. One mother described receiving her contact letter as 'warming'. Another said, 'When I see the letter, I am like a kid at Christmas. I get very excited and very emotional, obviously it is fantastic.' Some birth relatives referred more generally to being able to feel happy again, at least some of the time, in their day-to-day life.

Despite feeling the adoption had been a very difficult experience, some birth relatives felt that, in some ways, the experience had changed them for the better, for example, by making them stronger, less judgmental or more empathic towards others with problems. For example, one birth mother who had a history of being abused both as a child and an adult said, 'It has changed me because I now no longer let crap happen to me'.

Negative indicators

When some birth relatives talked about the adoption, they seemed over-whelmed with negative feelings about themselves, feelings of shame, worthlessness or guilt, and a focus on what they failed to do for their child. One birth mother said that the adoption had made her feel 'like you are no good for nothing'; a birth father said, 'I feel like I'm letting my girl down'. Another birth mother felt very guilty about the fact that, because of her actions, her whole family had lost the child. In other cases, birth relatives were strongly focused on what everyone else had done wrong – they argued they were completely blameless and seemed fixed in a state of intense anger. For example, one birth father used the word "abducted" to describe his child's adoption. In some cases, birth relatives described being unable to control feelings of anger or rage towards social services. One birth father described how, three years after his son's removal, he had 'totally lost it' with a social worker; throughout his interview he seemed preoccupied with bitterness towards this person and a desire for revenge. Another birth father said he would like to 'shoot the bastards [social workers]'. As we saw in Chapter 6, most birth relatives were opposed to the child's adoption, and so anger at professionals was widespread. Where it was seen as a contraindicator of coping with adoption was where this anger had an all-consuming quality in terms of its intensity or duration, and the person seemed unable to focus on much else.

Birth relatives coded as "low" on dealing with the impact of adoption on self were those who did not describe any change in their feelings over time, or who had no sense of hope that their feelings would ever change. For example, one grandmother said, 'Nothing is ever going to change the way I feel'; another birth mother said that the adoption had 'ruined her life' and that she would 'never get over it'. As we described earlier, for many birth relatives the removal of the child could precipitate a crisis often affecting their emotional and physical health and behaviour. We interviewed some people quite close to the time of the child's removal, and they appeared to be currently in this state of crisis. However, even some people we talked to some time after key events had taken place seemed to be still stuck in an acute phase of grieving. For example, one father we spoke to four years after the loss of his children described how he had not been able to regain any equilibrium since then:

I've started drinking a lot of alcohol... I fell out with a lot of people... Everything has sort of gone to pot... I have lost my muscle and have got a beer gut and to me I feel ashamed... I feel, I just think, "Well, sod it".

Where birth relatives reported they were currently suffering from acute symptoms of psychological distress related specifically to the adoption (e.g. depression, anxiety, nightmares, flashbacks), this was seen as a negative indicator. For example, one grandmother said that she had experienced two recent breakdowns, that she could not sleep and was having nightmares. She was unable to do work around the house because she had 'no incentive'. Her husband had left her and she could not forgive her son (the birth father) for 'having a hand' in her grandchild's adoption.

As with the birth father in the paragraph above, several people described using alcohol, drugs or "blocking out" strategies to avoid their pain. One birth mother said that she drank because 'It helps to numb the pain in my head'. Another birth father, who also used alcohol in this way, said, 'I just don't want to think about [my daughter]. I do anything to blank it out.' Other people described avoiding any contact with other children.

Being unable to act to improve their situation was seen as a negative indicator of dealing with the impact of adoption on self. For example, some people said that it was too difficult to share their problems with friends or professionals; one birth mother said she did not want to seek any support because 'they bring up my past and it just upsets me'. This feeling also isolated her from informal support networks – she said she would not make friends: 'They want to know the ins and outs and I don't want to talk about [the children]'. One birth mother said she wouldn't talk to anyone, 'not even my partner'. For some people, feelings of powerlessness got in the way of seeking or accepting help. Other people felt so unmotivated they could not act to establish contact with the child, even though they were desperate to hear how they were getting on. One birth mother said, 'I could make the move and phone to find out what is happening but I just find myself shutting it all out'.

Birth relatives coded as low on coping with the impact of adoption expressed no or almost no positive feelings about the adoption, not even when they heard about, or from their child. For example, one person described how 'it kills me that [the adoptive parents] have got the kids . . .' Although she looked forward to getting the letters, they actually reawakened her sense of loss and left her feeling devastated. Some people emphasised how they felt the adoption had changed them for the worse. For example, one birth father related how the adoption had made him 'cold and hard faced . . . nothing bothers me anymore the way it used to . . . I don't get happy and I don't really get sad. I don't even get angry . . . everything just seems grey all over'. A birth mother explained how she now avoids relationships: 'It's made me not want to deal with kids . . . I absolutely adore kids but it's made me not want to be around them . . . It's made me not able to [have a partner]'. A birth father described how he felt that adoption had 'changed my personality from being a decent person to being at first a wreck and now just paranoid . . . I'm so bitter and twisted.'

Results of coping with adoption ratings

Results for the three sub scales

We could not code the three dimensions of coping with adoption for all

Table 11.1
Ratings of acceptance of dual connection at Time 1 and Time 2

| | Time 1 | | Time 2 | |
	Number	*Percentage*	*Number*	*Percentage*
Very low	11	19.3	9	18.8
Low	9	15.8	7	14.6
Mixed	16	28.1	9	18.8
Mainly high	11	19.3	12	25.0
Very high	10	17.5	11	22.9
Total	**57**	**100.0**	**48**	**100.1**

birth relatives in the study. Where couples were interviewed together, ratings were made for only one person, based solely on their replies (we chose the person who said the most in the interview). "Accepting dual connection" and "feelings about the outcomes of adoption for the child" were only rated in cases where the child was placed for adoption, or was about to be placed. Occasionally, coding could not be undertaken because interview transcriptions were unclear in the relevant parts. The numbers of cases that were coded for each of the subscales are given in the following tables.

Table 11.1 shows the results of coding of acceptance of dual connection at Time 1 and Time 2. The results in this table show that scores on this dimension were fairly evenly spread across the range. The mean scores on this subscale at Time 1 and Time 2 respectively were 3 and 3.2.

Table 11.2 shows how birth relatives were coded on "feelings about the outcomes of adoption for the child" at Time 1 and Time 2. At Time 1, birth relatives were split roughly equally between the three groups. At Time 2, there were fewer people coded as negative and more coded as positive. Mean scores at Time 1 were 3.14 and at Time 2, 3.63.

Table 11.2
Feelings about the outcomes of adoption for the child

	Time 1		Time 2	
	Number	*Percentage*	*Number*	*Percentage*
1. Negative	16	28.1	7	14.6
3. Mixed	21	36.8	19	39.6
5. Positive	20	35.1	22	45.8
Total	**57**	**100.0**	**48**	**100.0**

Table 11.3 contains the data about how birth relatives were rated on "dealing with the impact of adoption on self". This shows that only a minority of birth relatives were scored as "positive" on this dimension at both points in time. Mean scores at Time 1 were 2.48 and at Time 2, 3.

Table 11.3
Dealing with the impact of adoption on self

	Time 1		Time 2	
	Number	*Percentage*	*Number*	*Percentage*
1. Negative	30	43.5	14	28.0
3. Mixed	27	39.1	22	44.0
5. Positive	12	17.4	14	28.0
Total	**69**	**100.0**	**50**	**100.0**

Creating a combined scale

The correlations between scores on each of the three different dimensions of coping with adoption were significant and positive but not so high as to suggest that they were measuring identical factors (correlations ranged from .55 to .68), and so scores from each of the three dimensions were combined to form one overall score called the "coping with adoption" scale. This was done by calculating the mean of the scores on the three separate dimensions in all cases where at least two of the three dimensions had been rated. Table 11.4 below shows the mean scores for the whole sample, broken down by birth relative type, at both points in time. A

Table 11.4
Means score on the "coping with adoption" combined scale for the whole sample and broken down by birth relative type

	Mean	*N*	*SD*
Whole sample T1	2.88	57	1.3
Whole sample T2	3.28	48	1.3
Birth mothers T1	2.92	37	1.3
Birth mothers T2	3.49	26	1.3
Birth fathers T1	2.57	14	1.0
Birth fathers T2	2.73	15	1.0
Grandparents T1	3.39	6	1.7
Grandparents T2	3.71	7	1.7

paired samples t-test (using the 41 cases where we had ratings at both points in time) was used to look at whether people's combined scores were different at the two points in time; scores at follow-up were significantly higher than at Time 1 ($t = -4.5$, $df = 40$, $p<.001$). The data in the table show that at both points in time the mean scores of birth fathers were lower than mothers or grandparents. However, a one way ANOVA showed no significant differences between the three groups of birth relatives at Time 1 (F ($df = 2$, 54) $= .87$, $p =.42$) or Time 2 (F ($df = 2$, 45) $= 2.16$, $p = 0.28$).

In order to look further at change over time, we created a new variable looking at the difference in mean scores on this scale. We calculated this by subtracting the Time 1 score from the Time 2 score. Thus, if the difference score was positive, that person's coping with adoption had improved, and if the difference score was negative, their coping with adoption had deteriorated. For the 41 people for whom we had scores at both points in time, seven people stayed the same (17%), seven people's coping scores had deteriorated (17%) and 27 people's scores had improved (56%). The mean difference in coping score for the whole sample was .54, a small improvement and the range was: -1 to 2.33.

The mean difference in coping scores for birth mothers (.69) and grandparents (.67) were very similar, but birth fathers' scores, although also generally showing improvement, were smaller (.21). An independent samples t-test comparing mean coping difference scores by gender showed that the difference between women and men (.69 versus .24) did not reach statistical significance ($t = -1.85$, $df = 39$, $p = .072$).

Summary

This chapter has reported the results of our analysis of how birth relatives were coping with the adoption at the time of interview. Key points are as follows:

* A measurement of "coping with adoption" was developed through a process of working with our birth relative consultant groups, drawing on previous theory and research, and studying the interviews with birth relatives in the study.

- In examining how birth relatives were coping with the loss of the child to adoption, three dimensions were examined: acceptance of dual connection; feelings about the outcomes of adoption for the child; and coping with the impact of adoption on self. Qualitative data illustrating how birth relatives were feeling/coping in these three areas are presented in the chapter.

- The three dimensions were rated using the whole of the interview with birth relatives. A coding handbook was developed that identified positive and negative indicators for each of these dimensions and all cases were rated at both points in time. Considerable variation between birth relatives in the current sample was found.

- Scores from the three separate dimensions were combined to form a mean overall "coping with adoption" score. Scores on this scale showed a small but significant improvement from Time 1 to Time 2.

- No significant differences in "coping with adoption" scores between the three groups of birth relatives were found, although there was a tendency for fathers to score lower than birth mothers and grandparents, and for fathers to improve less in their scores over time than other birth relatives.

12 The mental health of birth relatives

As we saw in Chapter 5, many birth relatives reported that mental ill health was one of the issues that they felt led to the child's adoption. Chapter 6 also showed that many birth relatives felt that their mental state was adversely affected by the adoption in both the short and long term, but particularly in the crisis period after the child's removal and before the adoption was finalised. In this chapter, we report birth relatives' scores on the Brief Symptom Inventory (BSI), the standardised measure used to assess mental distress.

Each of the 53 items on the BSI is rated by the individual on a five-point scale of distress from 0 (not at all) to four (extremely) – in relation to symptoms experienced in the last seven days. The results of the test can be examined at the level of individual items, the nine primary symptom dimensions, and, in addition, there are three global indices.

On the BSI, the primary symptom dimensions are:

1. Somatisation
2. Obsessive compulsive
3. Interpersonal sensitivity
4. Depression
5. Anxiety
6. Hostility
7. Phobic anxiety
8. Paranoid ideation
9. Psychoticism

The three global indices are:

- GSI: Global severity index (takes into account number of symptoms and intensity of distress)
- PST: Positive symptom total (number of symptoms reported)
- PSDI: Positive symptom distress index (an intensity measure corrected for number of symptoms – indicates average level of distress)

The BSI can also be used to identify which individuals are "case positive" (suggesting a clinically significant level of psychiatric symptoms) in terms of their psychological distress.

Norms have been established for four distinct samples: adult psychiatric outpatients; adult non-patients; adult psychiatric inpatients; and adolescent non-patients (Derogatis, 1993). The birth relative sample was compared to both adult non-patients and adult psychiatric outpatients.

Of the 73 birth relatives in the study, 68 completed the BSI at Time 1 (93%). These were 19 males and 51 females (41 birth mothers, 18 birth fathers, 8 grandmothers and 1 grandfather). Of the 57 birth relatives who took part at Time 2, 51 completed the measure (84%): (26 birth mothers, 17 birth fathers and 7 grandmothers, 1 grandfather.)

Results of the BSI for the whole sample

Table 12.1 shows the mean raw scores for two normative samples (adult non-patients and adult psychiatric outpatients) and for the birth relatives in the study at Time 1 and Time 2. This table shows that, at both points in time, birth relatives were evidencing exceptionally high levels of psychological distress compared to the non-patient comparison sample. Even compared to the adult psychiatric outpatient sample, birth relatives had higher means scores on every dimension except one (anxiety) at Time 1, and on four dimensions at Time 2. Birth relatives' scores on "paranoid ideation" seem particularly elevated, even in relation to the psychiatric outpatient sample. The symptoms included in this scale are:

- feeling others are to blame for most of your troubles;
- feeling that most people cannot be trusted;
- feeling that you are watched or talked about by others;
- feeling that others are not giving you proper credit for your achievements;
- feeling that people will take advantage of you if you let them.

These "symptoms" seem to fit very closely with how birth relatives told us it feels to have a child removed in compulsory adoption proceedings (see Chapter 6), in particular, the feeling that they are up against powerful and collusive forces of opposition. This begs the question as to whether

Table 12.1
Scores on the BSI compared to norms for patients and non-patients

	Mean – adult non-patients	Mean – adult psychiatric outpatient	Mean – birth relatives in the study	
			T1 (n = 68)	T2 (n = 51)
Somatisation	.29	.83	.97	.97
Obsessive compulsive	.43	1.57	1.59	1.46
Interpersonal sensitivity	.32	1.58	1.69	1.36
Depression	.28	1.80	1.83	1.48
Anxiety	.35	1.70	1.28	1.04
Hostility	.35	1.16	1.30	1.05
Phobic anxiety	.17	.86	1.13	.95
Paranoid ideation	.34	1.14	1.96	1.77
Psychoticism	.15	1.19	1.34	1.20
GSI	.30	1.32	1.47	1.26
PDSI	1.29	2.14	2.45	2.33
PST	11.45	30.80	29.92	26.29

birth relatives report such experiences of adoption because they are in a paranoid state of mind, or is it that they are realistically describing experiences of disempowerment? If the latter is the case, then "paranoid ideation" for this sample of people may not have the same meaning in terms of psychiatric symptoms as for other groups, be they patients or non-patients. Either way, service providers have to try and engage birth relatives who feel everyone is against them and who lack trust in others.

Individuals are "case positive" if the T score (a standardised score) of their GSI – Glocal Severity Index – is greater than or equal to 63 (indicating they are in the highest 10% of scores), or if any two primary dimension T scores are greater than or equal to 63. Of the 68 people who completed the measure at Time 1, 54 (79%) were "case positive". At Time 2, 38 of the 51 birth relatives were case positive (74.5%).

Results of the BSI by birth relative type

Table 12.2 reports how many birth relatives were case positive by birth relative type. Over three-quarters of both mothers and fathers were case positive at both points in time. It is hard to attribute much to the figures for grandparents because the numbers are so small, but three grandparents were doing much better at Time 2 than at Time 1.

Table 12.2
Percentages of birth relatives who were "case positive"

	T1 case positive		*T2 case positive*	
	N	*%*	*N*	*%*
Birth mothers	32	78	20	77
Birth fathers	14	78	13	76.5
Grandmothers	8	89	5	62.5

Table 12.3 shows the Global Severity Index (GSI) raw scores and T scores for birth mothers, birth fathers and grandmothers at both time points (the data from the one grandfather is not included in this table). The raw scores for birth fathers are lower than those for mothers and grandmothers. However, women's scores on the BSI are typically higher than men's and so the T scores provide a more useful comparison; these suggest very little difference between the scores for mothers and fathers at either point in time. Grandmothers have almost identical T scores to mothers and fathers at Time 1, and slightly lower scores at Time 2. As noted above, three of seven grandmothers had improved significantly by follow up. ANOVAs were used to compare the T scores of fathers, mothers and grandparents at Time 1 and Time 2. No significant differences were found (Time 1: $F = .13$, $n = 68$, $df = 2$, $p = .87$; Time 2: $F = .90$, $n = 51$, $df = 2$, $p = .41$).

THE MENTAL HEALTH OF BIRTH RELATIVES

Table 12.3
Global Severity Index scores for birth mothers, birth fathers and birth grandmothers

	Birth mothers		Birth fathers		Grandmothers	
	T1	*T2*	*T1*	*T2*	*T1*	*T2*
	(n = 41)	*(n = 26)*	*(n = 18)*	*(n = 17)*	*(n = 8)*	*(n = 7)*
GSI mean raw score	1.64	1.46	1.08	1.11	1.36	1.09
GSI mean t score	68.93	66.77	67.28	67.35	67.00	59.71

Changes in GSI scores over time

Forty-eight people completed the measure at both points in time and 33 of these (69%) were case positive at both points in time (i.e. they had clinically significant levels of symptoms at baseline and follow-up). Six people (13%) moved from being case positive to case negative (indicating *improved* mental health), four people (8%) remained case negative at both points in time and five people (10%) who were case negative at Time 1 were case positive at Time 2 (their mental health had *deteriorated*). A paired samples t-test was used to compare the GSI raw scores of birth relatives at Time 1 and Time 2. Although the mean score was lower (indicating improvement) at follow-up, the difference did not quite reach statistical significance ($t = 1.9$, $df = 47$, $p = .06$).

In order to look further at changes in mental health over time, we created a new variable looking at the difference in mean scores on the GSI raw scores. We calculated this by subtracting the Time 1 score from the Time 2 score. On this measure, higher scores suggest more problems, and so, if the difference score was positive that person's psychological distress had increased, and if the difference score was negative their psychological distress had decreased. For the 48 people who completed the measure at both points in time, one person stayed the same (2%); 21 people's scores were positive, indicating deterioration (44%); and 26 people's scores were negative, indicating improvement (54%). The mean difference in GSI score for the whole sample was –.23, and the range was –2.7 to 1.09.

The mean difference in coping scores for birth mothers was –.28; for grandparents it was –.56; and for birth fathers it was –0.001. No significant differences in mean GSI change scores were found either by birth relative type ($F = 1.26$, $df = 2$, $p = .29$) or by gender ($t = .96$, $df = 46$, $p = .34$).

Summary

This chapter has reported the results of the analysis of the mental health of birth relatives, measured using a standardised questionnaire, the Brief Symptom Inventory. Key findings are as follows:

- The scores of birth relatives on the BSI were very high, indicating high levels of psychological distress. Scores on all nine symptom dimensions of this measure, and on the three global indices, were very similar to, or greater than, the scores for a psychiatric outpatient comparison sample.
- There was a lot of correspondence between the symptoms that birth relatives were experiencing that were evidenced in the BSI and the feelings they described in relation to their experiences of compulsory adoption.
- The subscale of this measure that was the most elevated compared to comparison samples was "paranoid ideation". There is much similarity between the symptoms that make up this subscale, and the feelings of disempowerment, anger, and suspicion of others that birth relatives described.
- Three-quarters of birth relatives in the study were experiencing psychological distress at clinically significant levels at both points in time.
- No significant differences were found between birth mothers, birth fathers and grandparents.
- Although there was a modest fall in the Global Severity Index mean score over time, the difference in scores between Time 1 and Time 2 was not statistically significant and for most people (69%), levels of distress remained at clinically significant levels.

13 The costs of providing support services

This chapter reports the findings of the costing of birth relative support services. The provision of support services by support workers is described, and estimates of the time spent providing such services and the subsequent cost of this provision are outlined. Finally, estimates of the use of services by birth relatives in the study, and ultimately the total cost of service provision for the "average" birth relative, are presented.

Case worker diaries

Twenty-four case workers from six of the eight participating agencies (two LAs, three ASAs and one VAA) agreed to complete the case worker time diaries. The majority of respondents were female ($n = 21$). Eight respondents described their role as a support (or project) worker, six described themselves as (senior) social workers, while others reported themselves to be administrators ($n = 4$), managers ($n = 3$) or counsellors ($n = 3$).

Ten respondents were employed full-time, and they averaged 36 hours of work each week (range: 35–37.5). Nine respondents were part-time, working an average of 24 hours per week (range: 16–30). Five case workers who completed the time diaries were self-employed, working an average of 19 hours per week (range: 7–35).

Table 13.1 reports the results of the aggregation of all respondents' time diaries, displaying (in minutes) the mean amount of time workers spent on different birth relative support activities (details of how these activities were defined for caseworkers completing the diaries is given in Chapter 3). It is evident from the table that most of the respondents ($n = 19$) provided counselling and therapeutic support, while contact support was only provided by about a third of people ($n = 9$). In terms of time commitment, the analysis suggests that a "session" of counselling and therapeutic support takes an average of 115 minutes to organise and deliver. An average contact support session takes less than an hour (47 minutes), while other support which is service-user focused takes just over an hour (69 minutes), and general and practical support takes 95 minutes.

Table 13.1
Time commitment for each birth relative support activity (minutes)

	N	Mean (in minutes)
Counselling & therapeutic support	19	115
Contact support	9	47
General & practical support	13	95
Other support – service-user focused	11	69
Other support – not service-user focused	11	116

The nature of the data collection tool allowed for a comparison of direct and indirect time commitments. Direct time was the time the worker actually spent meeting with the service user or talking with them on the telephone. Indirect time included activities related to facilitating the support (for example, case recording, administration, liaising with colleagues, travelling, email or letter contact with service users). Table 13.2 presents the split of time commitments between direct and indirect work. The indirect time commitments were in every instance greater than the direct time commitments. For example, when providing counselling and therapeutic support, a case worker spent, on average, 54 minutes of their total time directly with a service user, and 79 minutes on indirect work; in effect, only 41% of the time was spent meeting with the service user, the majority (59%) was spent preparing and organising the support, or maybe travelling to make a home visit.

Valuing resource use
The average time commitments for the different support activities presented in Table 13.1 above were valued using the unit cost of one hour of service user-related work. The resulting unit costs of providing each specific service are presented in Table 13.3.

Table 13.2

Average direct and indirect time commitment for each support activity (minutes)

	N	*Mean (in minutes)*
Counselling & therapeutic support		
Total direct	17	54
Total indirect	16	79
Contact support		
Total direct	5	27
Total indirect	7	42
General & practical support		
Total direct	9	55
Total indirect	11	67
Other support – service-user focused		
Total direct	7	51
Total indirect	8	50
Other support – not service-user focused		
Total direct	1	143
Total indirect	10	113

Table 13.3

Unit costs of birth relative support services (£ sterling, 2007 prices)

	Cost
Counselling & therapeutic support	74.50
Contact support	30.78
General & practical support	61.67
Other support – service-user focused	44.68
Other support – not service-user focused	75.28

Service use diaries

Sixty-five completed service use diaries were returned. In these diaries workers in the agencies kept a record of all the activities they had undertaken in supporting individual birth relatives in the study over a 12-month period. There were a number of couples in the study, and in some instances, two diaries were completed, one for the birth mother and one for the birth father, but in other instances, only one diary was completed for the couple as a whole. From these diaries it was not always obvious whether the support was given to the couple together or separately; in one instance, there were initially similar visits to the birth mother and father, but then the birth mother had more visits. Given that case workers were asked to complete a diary for each individual in the study, for consistency we have assumed that all couples were seen separately, that is individually, by the case worker (e.g. if one diary was returned for a couple, then the service use was duplicated for both individuals). As such we have resource use information for 69 individuals in the sample, and missing data for only four individuals.

Resource use

Resource use over a 12-month period as recorded in the service use diaries is described and summarised in Table 13.4. The table shows that, in terms of specific services, the "average" birth relative received: 1.49 information and advice services; 0.71 support group sessions; 1.43 counselling sessions; assistance with indirect contact 1.36 times; and 1.26 sessions of casework over a 12-month period. The use of services providing needs assessment was minimal, while no birth relative received therapy or advocacy services. This may be because support workers define these activities quite formally. For example, a worker may interpret therapy as an activity undertaken by somebody with a specific therapeutic qualification, for example, a psychotherapist or a cognitive behavioural therapist. No birth relatives were reported by their support worker to have been provided with help for face-to-face contact. This is not surprising as very few birth relatives in the interview sample had face-to-face contact with their child. Furthermore, as we saw in the mapping survey

(Chapter 2), responsibility for supporting face-to-face contact tends to be retained by the placing local authority.

Table 13.4 also shows that there were a large number of "other" services provided, described as emotional support, life story work, and liaising with the local authority. To aid the costing of services, each specific "other" service was (where possible) re-categorised to fit within the categorisation of support services provided by case workers (e.g. emotional support was recoded as counselling).

In total, the "average" birth relative received 8.34 services/sessions over a 12-month period. This ranged from 0 to 70. Thirty-two per cent (*n* = 22) of the sample received no services or support during the 12-

Table 13.4
Summary of resource use by birth relatives over a 12-month period (n = 69)

	Mean	*Standard deviation*	*Minimum*	*Maximum*
Needs assessment	0.13	0.54	0	4
Information and advice	1.49	3.62	0	17
Support groups	0.71	2.62	0	18
Therapy	0	0	0	0
Counselling	1.43	3.94	0	20
Assistance with direct (face-to-face) contact	0	0	0	0
Assistance with letterbox contact (indirect)	1.36	2.53	0	10
Casework	1.26	4.55	0	28
Advocacy	0	0	0	0
Other	1.96	5.77	0	34
Total service provision	8.34	14.54	0	70

month period. Nineteen people (28%) received between 1 and 5 sessions/ services and 20 people (30%) had between 6 and 18 services. Twelve people (17%) used 19 or more services – this figure includes three people who used 50 or more services. This skewness means the data were not normally distributed and it may be more informative to consider the median value (which is two), although in general, economists are more interested in mean values. The mean numbers of services used, after excluding non-users, was 12.26 services. However, given that the "average" or typical birth relative includes individuals who are offered services but do not take them up, it is important to include these non-users in the mean estimations.

Caseworkers also recorded the number of planned but missed appointments, so called "did not attends" or DNAs. In the sample of 69 birth relatives, there were 28 DNAs over the 12-month period. The total number of sessions by the sample as a whole was 576, so five per cent were missed. The inclusion of these missed appointments in the estimation of the mean would result in an average of 8.75 sessions per birth relative.

Total costs of providing birth relative support services

The average birth relative received 8.34 services in a 12-month period; these were estimated to cost £511. The range was £0 to £4,563 and the interquartile range (the middle 50% of the sample) was £0 to £524, reflecting the fact that a number of birth relatives received no services. When only those individuals who used services were included, the average cost of providing birth relative support services over a 12-month period rose to £751. Similar caveats exist regarding this estimate, as discussed above.

The inclusion of planned but missed visits in the calculation of total cost gives a slightly higher average cost of £540 per birth relative. This is, however, an overestimate as although these visits were planned, and so incurred indirect costs, they did not actually take place, so no direct cost was incurred. If direct costs are assumed to contribute around 40 per cent of all costs, then the inclusion of the missed appointments would only increase the average cost to around £528. In the subsequent analyses of cost and resource use below, the inclusion or otherwise of missed appointments has no influence on the findings, so for the sake of simplicity, missed appointments were excluded.

In order to explore whether there were any differences between agencies in the resources/costs incurred by birth relatives in the study, we compared the three largest participating agencies (ASA 1, ASA 2 and ASA 4) from whom most of the sample were drawn (55 of the 69 cases – 80 per cent – for whom service use diaries were completed). Table 13.5 reports these figures. The table shows that the numbers of birth relatives who, according to the agency, had not used any services nor incurred any costs during the 12-month study period varied: 11 of the 23 individuals who were referred by ASA 1, and seven of the individuals referred by ASA 2 received no services (resource use = 0, cost = £0), whereas only two of the individuals referred by ASA 4 were recorded as using no services. The Kruksal-Wallis test (chosen because the data were not normally distributed so ANOVA could not be used) showed significant differences between the three agencies in terms of costs ($H = 12.2$, $df = 2$, $p<.01$) and services ($H = 11.3$, $df = 2$, $p<.01$).

Table 13.5
Total resource use and total cost for three largest contributing ASAs

	N	Resource use		Cost	
		Mean	Range	Mean	Range
ASA 1	23	3.39	0–20	£185.61	£0–£999.10
ASA 2	19	5.68	0–52	£352.75	£0–£3,527.54
ASA 4	13	22.77	0–70	£1,393.23	£0–£4,562.88
Total sample	69	8.35	0–70	£5,11.52	£0–£4,562.88

To understand the potential influence of non-service users, subsequent analysis compared costs and resource use whilst excluding the zero values (i.e. the individuals who did not use any services). The results of this are presented in Table 13.6 below. This shows that service users of ASA 4 still have a greater level of service provision ($H = 9.9$, $df = 2$, $p<0.01$) and incur more costs ($H = 11.45$, $df = 2$, $p<.01$). Even when the extreme values (service use ≥ 40) were excluded from the analysis, ASA 4 service users still had a higher use and higher cost of services. Service take up in this agency was generally very high (see Table 4.2), and they did have a large proportion of self-referrals (see Table 4.4), which may mean their service users were more motivated to engage fully with the services on offer. Eight of the service users of this agency also had access to a greater number of services than are usually offered, because one branch of this organisation had a special initiative in operation at the time of our study. Caution should be exercised when interpreting these results; ASA 4 is a large agency and the 13 individuals included in this costing analysis represent only a small proportion of their birth relative service users.

Table 13.6
Total resource use and total cost for the three largest contributing ASAs – excluding non-service users

	N	Resource use		Cost	
		Mean	Range	Mean	Range
ASA 1	12	6.50	1–20	£355.75	£61.67–£999.10
ASA 2	12	9.00	1–52	£588.51	£30.78–£3,527.54
ASA 4	11	26.91	2–70	£1,646.55	£136.17–£4,562.88

The relationship between self-reported service use and resource use and cost

In order to explore the extent to which agency reported service use corresponded with birth relative reported service use, we looked at the agency reported costs and services alongside the categories of service use generated from the interview data. Table 13.7 reports the relationship between self-reported use of services and that recorded by case workers during the 12-month period. The table shows the difference in costs between the four overall categories of service use identified in the interviews (regular users; brief or sporadic users; non-users who knew about services; and non-users who did not know about services). As would be expected, regular service users used the most services, and incurred the highest costs. People who reported using no services and having no knowledge of them used fewest services and incurred the least costs. Little difference is apparent between brief or sporadic service users and those who knew about services but did not use them (many of whom might have had some initial contact with the agency). Differences are also apparent between the two categories of regular and brief service users versus non-users.

While there clearly is correspondence between agency reported service use and birth relative reported service use, the two data sources did not entirely match up. For example, despite some individuals reporting to be regular service users in the interviews, seven individuals were recorded as having no service use in the service use diaries. This could suggest they were receiving support from elsewhere, or it could be that the services they reported receiving were received either before or after the 12-month period over which agencies supplied data. Similarly, three individuals that self-reported no service use were identified in the service use diaries as using services. This could reflect some form of self-report-

Table 13.7
Self-reported use of support services and resource use, cost (n = 64)

	Resource count *Mean (range)*	*Total cost (£)* *Mean (range)*
Summary of self-reported support (4 groups)		
Regular service	13.59 (0, 70)	869.29 (0, 4563)
Brief or sporadic	4.67 (0, 10)	241.09 (0, 555)
Know, but did not use	3.81 (0, 18)	213.54 (0, 1079)
None, no knowledge		
of services	1.67 (0, 6)	74.03 (0, 259)
Summary of self-reported support (2 groups)		
Regular/brief	10.74 (0, 70)	668.80 (0, 4563)
Not used	3.23 (0, 18)	175.50 (0, 1079)

ing bias, for example, a birth relative may have forgotten that they had used services. Alternatively, it could be that the agency had invested resources, and incurred costs, in attempting to offer a service (e.g. writing letters or making home visits) that the individual never took up.

Summary

This chapter has reported the results of the costing of birth relative support services. Key findings are as follows:

- A process of bottom-up costing was used to estimate the costs of a range of activities provided by support workers employed to provide support services to birth relatives. These unit costs were then used to value the support services provided to birth relatives over a 12-month period.
- The "average" birth relative was estimated to have used 8.35 support services. These average figures included a number of individuals who used no services. As was shown in Chapter 4, many birth relatives who were referred to support services did not take up the offer; as such it is important to include these individuals in the estimation of the average, as they contribute to our understanding of a "typical" birth relative.
- The specific services used by birth relatives included information and advice, counselling, letterbox contact and casework. No support worker recorded that they provided therapy, advocacy, or assistance with face-to-face contact to any individual in the study.
- The "average" birth relative was estimated to cost £511 over the 12-month period. This included a number of individuals who incurred no cost (as they did not use any services) and some users who utilised considerably the services that were on offer; the maximum cost was £4,563.
- There were significant differences between the three largest ASAs participating in the study in terms of the services provided to birth relatives and the costs of these. In particular, one ASA provided significantly more services at greater cost to its service users, even when non-service users were excluded from the analysis.

- Most individuals that self reported having used services had higher recorded resource use and subsequently higher costs, but sometimes the self reported use did not match with the recorded use. This may be a timing issue as the interviews asked about "any" use and the service use diaries were for a specific 12-month period, or it may be an issue of reporting bias. It also may indicate that agencies incur costs in attempting to engage service users who do not respond.

14 Costs and resource use, self-reported service use and the outcomes of support for birth relatives

This chapter presents the results of the statistical analyses exploring the relationship between both agency-reported and self-reported service use and a range of outcomes for birth relatives.

In these analyses, the key **independent (predictor) variables** that were used are as follows:

- individual costs of birth relatives (the individual cost in pounds sterling of services that each birth relative used over a 12-month period) (see Chapter 13);
- individual agency reported resource use by birth relatives (this is the number of services/sessions that each birth relative used over a 12-month period) (see Chapter 13);
- the five individual types of service provision identified from interviews (emotional support, help with contact, advice and information, advocacy and liaison, group support) (see Chapter 7);
- the total number of the above five services that each birth relative reported receiving from one to five (see Chapter 7);
- the two categories of service users ("regular users and brief and sporadic users" and "non-users") (see Chapter 7).

The first two of these independent variables are the agency reported service use variables (also referred to as the economic variables), and the last three are the self reported service use variables.

The key **dependent (outcome) variables** that are used are as follows:

Satisfaction
- Birth relatives' satisfaction with services (see Chapter 8). Birth relatives were categorised as being either "primarily positive", "mixed

or neutral" or "primarily negative" about the support services they had received. Because the numbers of people in the latter two categories were small, they were combined into one group. Birth relatives who were primarily positive about services are described as "satisfied" and those who were "mixed or neutral" or "primarily negative" as "unsatisfied". These ratings were applied only to birth relatives who said they had used services.

Mental health outcomes as measured on the Brief Symptom Inventory (BSI) (see Chapter 12).

- "Caseness" on the BSI: Birth relatives were classified as being "case positive" on the BSI if they reported distressing psychological symptoms at a clinically significant level (see Chapter 12 for details of how this was defined).
- Raw scores on the BSI Global Severity Index (GSI): The global severity index scores take account of both the number of distressing psychological symptoms people reported, and the intensity of these. When looking at this outcome in relation to self-reported service use, we have used each birth relatives' "last" GSI score (i.e. for most people this was their Time 2 score, but for those people who did not take part at Time 2 their Time 1 score was used as this corresponded time-wise with their self-reported service use data).
- "Change" scores on the GSI: For people who completed the BSI at both waves, Time 1 scores were subtracted from Time 2 scores to create a new variable indicating the change in the scores over time. Negative scores indicate an improvement in mental health.

"Coping with adoption" outcomes (see Chapter 11)
- Birth relatives' scores on the combined "coping with adoption" scale: This was the mean score across the three sub-scales of this measure (accepting dual connection, satisfaction with the child's life in the adoptive family, dealing with the impact of adoption on self). When analysing self-reported service use, we used people's "last" coping score.
- Change in coping scores: Time 1 combined coping scores were sub-

tracted from Time 2 coping scores to create a new variable indicating changes in coping over time. Positive values indicated an improvement in coping.

Summary of results of statistical analyses

A number of statistical analyses were carried out which explored whether the use of services was related to outcomes.[1] Below, the key conclusions from these analyses are summarised.

Satisfaction with services used

- The number of different types of services that birth relatives said they had used predicted whether birth relatives were satisfied with their service provision, with those birth relatives who had used a broader range of services being more likely to be satisfied. A logistic regression showed that, for each one further type of service birth relatives said they had used, they were more than twice as likely to be satisfied with their services overall ($\chi^2 = 7.14$, $N = 48$, $df = 1$, $p < .01$, odds ratio = 2.12).

- Two particular types of service were significantly associated with satisfaction with services: advice and information ($\chi^2 = 6.9$, $df = 1$, $p < .01$), and emotional support ($\chi^2 = 6.1$, $df = 1$, $p < .05$). Birth relatives who reported receiving these services were significantly more likely to be satisfied with their service provision than birth relatives who did not report receiving these types of service.

- Neither the number of services that people had used, nor the cost of these services, predicted satisfaction with service provision.

Mental health outcomes

- There was evidence that agency-reported resource use and costs were significantly related to *improvements* in mental health over time: the more services people used, and the higher the cost of these, the greater was people's improvement in mental health (resource use: $r = -0.38$,

---

[1] Full details of the results of all the statistical analyses carried out are available on request from the first author.

$p<.01$, $N = 46$; cost: $r = -0.37$, $p <.05$, $N = 46$). The correlation is unable to address the issue of causation, but it does provide evidence of a link between service use and improving mental health.

- When we looked at self-reported service use (service users versus non users) and the change in GSI scores over time, we found the same pattern as with the agency-reported service use (i.e. those who had used services improved more than those who did not), although results did not reach statistical significance ($t = -1.29$, $df = 46$, $p = .2$).
- No significant relationship was found between the number of different types of services that people used and their mental health outcomes.
- There was no strong evidence that birth relatives' levels of mental health problems were significantly related to their take-up of services. Birth relatives who had very high levels of mental health problems (i.e. they were "case positive" on the BSI) did not subsequently use a significantly different amount of services/costs than those who were case negative. Similarly, when people who had used services were compared to those who had not used services, no differences in their GSI scores were found. No significant associations were found between GSI scores and costs and services used.

Coping with adoption
- Birth relatives who reported they had used services had significantly higher coping scores than those who had not used services.[2] A limitation of these results is that we cannot know the direction of effect – whether receiving services promoted coping, or whether the ability to cope to a certain extent enabled birth relatives to receive services.
- Women's coping scores were significantly higher than men's ($F = 4.7$, $N = 62$, $df = 1$, $p < .05$.) There was some indication (not quite reaching statistical significance: $F = 3.6$, $p = .06$) of an interaction between gender, service use, and coping with adoption in that men who had not used services had lower coping scores than men who had; for women

---

[2] A two way ANOVA was used and gender was included as a fixed factor. Birth relatives who used services had significantly higher coping scores than those who had not ($F = 5.4$, $N = 62$, $df = 1$, $p < .05$). The effect size was medium-large (partial eta squared = .09).

there was very little difference in coping scores of service users compared with non-users.

- Looking at self-reported service use, a significant positive correlation between the number of different types of services people reported they had received and their coping with adoption scores was found, indicating that the more types of services people had used, the better they were coping with adoption ($r = .30$, $N = 62$, $p <. 05$). A limitation of these results is that we do not know whether higher levels of coping enabled birth relatives to access a broader range of services, or whether a broader range of services facilitated high levels of coping.
- There were no significant differences in changes in coping scores of people who had used services compared with those who had not. Changes in coping scores were positively correlated with higher costs and resource use, although this was not statistically significant ($p = .12$) and therefore could have occurred by chance.

Summary

- For almost all the outcomes we looked at, people using services (or using more services) seemed to be somewhat better off than people not using them (or using fewer services). There was some evidence that birth relative support services were having a positive impact on those people using them. Improvement in mental health over time was significantly related to resource use and cost; and people who had used services were coping significantly better than those who had not.
- The findings in this chapter give some indication about the relationship between the nature of support services and outcomes. The provision of a greater number of different types of support activities was related to satisfaction, and to higher levels of coping with adoption. Emotional support and advice and information were associated with service user satisfaction.
- Many analyses yielded no statistically significant results. This may be because of the severity, complexity and longevity of people's problems and the brevity of the follow-up, and because sample sizes were too small to detect any except large effects (Cohen, 1992). It is also likely

that outcomes, such as people's mental health and coping with adoption, were affected by a broad range of factors and not just by the support they received from the agency. Other important factors are likely to be contact with the adopted child, the availability of support from other sources, and individual factors associated with resilience, including people's levels of functioning before the loss of the child to adoption.

15 Discussion of findings

This research set out to add to what is currently known about the practice of supporting birth relatives through and after adoption. It was commissioned to explore issues relating to the implementation of the Adoption and Children Act 2002. This Act contained important changes in the provision of support services for birth relatives of adopted children, recognising the lifelong impact of adoption upon them.

The research explored a number of questions relating to:

- the availability and organisational sources of support services;
- the referral of birth relatives to these support services and their take up;
- birth relatives' experiences of compulsory adoption;
- the types of services provided to birth relatives and their experiences of these; and
- the cost and outcomes of birth relative support services.

The study employed both qualitative and quantitative methods to answer these questions. Detailed findings have been presented in each chapter. This discussion therefore focuses on the following key themes: an evaluation of the strengths and limitations of the research; the needs of the birth relatives; the experience of adoption support services; and the role of children's services in supporting birth relatives. Particular issues relating to birth fathers were apparent throughout the analysis and these are also considered. The relevance of birth relative support services to the ongoing welfare of adopted children is also discussed and the chapter concludes by summarising implications for practice.

Evaluation of the strengths and limitations of the research

Strengths
- Data were collected from practitioners and agencies in the mapping

study. We had collected resource use data from agencies, and we had the personal perspectives of birth relatives and a standardised measure of their mental health. Using these multiple sources of data, we were able to triangulate information and combine qualitative and quantitative methodologies.

- The target sample of birth relatives (a hard to reach group), representative of birth relatives generally referred to services, was recruited and there was good retention from Time 1 to Time 2. This may indicate something not just about the successful approach of the research team but about birth relatives' desire to tell their side of the story.

- The strong focus on birth relatives' perspectives is a key strength of the study. To effectively support this group of people, we need to know their reactions to the adoption of the child – and birth relatives' voices are not often heard.

- Birth relative consultants were successfully involved in the research process at three stages: the planning of data collection and recruitment, data analysis, and understanding implications for practice. Innovative methods for involving service users were used and this project is an example of collaborative research (Hanley, 2003).

Limitations

- There are other perspectives that are not included, most importantly those of adopted children and adoptive parents.

- We were not able to identify and compare different models of birth relative support. However, given that the study began only at the time when the new legislation came fully into force, it is unsurprising that we did not find services that had developed specific models of intervention. It may be that future research could compare different models of service delivery, for example, initiatives that use specific therapeutic or other types of intervention models, and comparisons of in-house local authority services with independent services.

- The cost predictions are likely to underestimate the true cost of providing birth relative support services, as recent research suggests that one component of the cost, overheads, has been traditionally undervalued in the standard costing literature (Selwyn et al, 2009).

- Although the sample of birth relatives was sufficient for the qualitative analysis we undertook, in terms of some of the quantitative analyses, the sample size may have been too small to detect anything except large effects (Cohen, 1992). Hence many of our analyses of the impact of support services on birth relatives are inconclusive.

Birth relatives' needs

Any support service must take account of the needs of its users. This research suggests four particular areas of need for the birth relatives of adopted children, these being: preceding problems; needs related to the adoption *process*; needs related to the loss of the child; and needs related to the social context of the adoption.

Preceding problems

The birth relatives' accounts of how their children came to be adopted revealed the range and complexity of the psychosocial problems these families faced. Against a backdrop of poverty (the employment rate amongst the sample was only 18%), the birth relatives contended with a wide range of complex and chronic difficulties, often related to lifelong problems with relationships. The most commonly cited issues were relationship difficulties, mental health problems and substance misuse. The co-existence and severity of the problems described suggest that adoption support services must take account of the complex needs of birth relatives who may be hard to engage. The diversity of the problems cited suggests that multiple strategies may be needed to engage service users with different needs.

The majority of the birth parents acknowledged that there were problems in their families, with only 10 per cent denying any difficulties at the time that their children were taken into care. Although the vast majority opposed the plan for adoption (87%), two-thirds of birth relatives (67%) agreed that the child was at risk of serious harm. The amount of detail that the birth relatives supplied, and the evident emotion with which they told their stories, suggest that an important support need is for their experiences to be heard and acknowledged. In the present research, there was a great deal of complexity in the way that birth relatives constructed the narrative about the child's adoption. It was clearly difficult and painful for some people to acknowledge the role they may have played in causing the child harm and some people appeared to defend against this difficulty by remaining intransigently angry and blaming others. The difficulty for birth relatives in understanding their problems and the impact of these on their children suggests that, for many people, anger, guilt and shame will be ongoing issues.

Needs related to the adoption process

The interview data support the view that the adoption process compounds the pre-existing difficulties of the birth relatives and many described a period of crisis. A research study carried out by After Adoption spoke of birth relatives' lives 'spiralling out of control' (2007, p 13). This crisis can be triggered at different times for different people depending on how particular events are interpreted. The accounts were characterised by intense emotion, including despair and rage. This could be accompanied by extreme behaviour including self-harm, substance misuse and suicide attempts. It is a time when the birth relative may be extremely vulnerable or at risk. The crisis period was a strong theme emerging from the interviews, and suggests the need for support to be offered early in the adoption process and for it to be offered repeatedly since the birth relatives varied in terms of their reactions to particular events.

This period of crisis often coincided with the need for the birth relative to be functioning well with parenting assessments and court proceedings underway. When they needed to be most together, they found themselves falling apart. If support services come in after the child is placed for adoption, this may be too late: the crisis that adoption can precipitate may disable birth parents from taking part constructively in subsequent processes. Some birth parents effectively disempower themselves in this crisis period. They may be confused and unable to take in information or unable to contain their anger enough to participate in important meetings. The need for independent support early in the process is indicated. The adoption process itself is experienced as confusing and disempowering. This partly reflects the reality of the legal process, which is drawn out and involves a series of judgements that systematically disempower the parent before permanently curtailing their legal relationship with the child. The birth parent has to negotiate this intimidating process at a time of personal crisis. The child's social worker may be unavoidably viewed as an adversary since he or she is arguing that it is not in the child's interests to remain with the birth relative. However skilful and respectful the worker, they are not in a position to adequately support the birth relative.

Needs related to the loss of the child

Birth relatives are often ill-equipped in terms of coping strategies and support networks to cope with the loss of their child. The high levels of psychological distress that birth relatives reported as a reaction to adoption were substantiated by the high levels of distress registered in the Brief Symptom Inventory scores.

Birth relatives' levels of mental distress was comparable to that experienced by psychiatric outpatients and levels of distress were high at both time points; however, relatively few birth relatives reported an ongoing involvement with mental health services. This highlights the need for support.

Adoption is an experience of profound loss for the birth relative. Many compared it to bereavement but one which lacked closure. Their descriptions of the emotions experienced echoed the findings of previous research on relinquishing parents (Winkler and Van Keppel, 1984; Bouchier et al, 1991; Howe et al, 1992; Wells, 1994). We found great variation within our sample in how birth relatives were coping with adoption. Most of the birth relatives were struggling to cope with the psychological challenges the adoption had brought about. However, some people seemed to have made no progress while other birth relatives showed remarkable evidence of recovery. The three separate dimensions in the "coping with adoption" measure were significantly correlated with each other. We saw in the interviews how the separate dimensions related to each other, for example, how positive news about the child's welfare could help birth relatives feel better about the child having a place within the adoptive family.

Needs related to the social context

Half of the birth relatives reported problems in getting support from friends and family. Adoption was an issue which could bring couples together in a minority of cases, but which contributed in several cases to driving them apart. Partners may have different coping strategies, with one partner needing to talk and the other wanting to avoid the issue. Grandparents, in particular, spoke of the difficulty of handling their own grief process in isolation, whilst also trying to support their offspring. In some families, birth relatives were ostracised by other members of the family who blamed them for the loss of the child; in others, the birth relative interviewed felt that more support from their extended family would have resulted in a different solution for the child. There were few sources of informal support outside the family because of the stigma attached to adoption. While the context of adoption has changed, with far fewer women compelled to relinquish their babies, the issue of stigma endures. Howe *et al* (1992) explore the notion of spoiled identity derived from Goffman (1963) and suggest that relinquishing mothers are stigmatised for transgressing social rules and failing in the socially valued role of mother. The concept of disenfranchised grief (Doka, 2002) is helpful in understanding how stigma and loss intersect. Disenfranchised grief refers to a loss which is not socially recognised and cannot be openly acknowledged. The grieving process may be compromised because of the lack of social support and acknowledgement of the loss. Understanding the social context of adoption underlines the need for support services since it highlights the difficulties that birth relatives have in finding informal support amongst their family and community networks.

The birth relatives of minority ethnicity who took part in our study did not identify particular needs for support related to their ethnicity. Although our sample had a reasonably representative proportion of birth relatives of minority ethnicity, the numbers of such people taking part was small and by no means representative of the diversity of birth relatives from minority ethnic groups. For example, our sample did not include people whose first language was not English. Recent research by Selwyn *et al* (2010) has identified the role of *izzat* (or family honour) in the adoption of children from some Asian families, this serving as an impetus for parents to relinquish or abandon their children. Similarly, a survey by Neil (2000) found that some Asian mothers were giving up their babies for adoption because of the stigma of illegitimacy within their communities; in some cases, women had concealed the birth of their child from friends and family. Where children are adopted in such circumstances, fears of people finding out about the adoption may make it extremely difficult for parents to participate in post-adoption contact or access birth relative support services, and services that can meet the needs of such parents need to be developed.

Service provision

Referral of birth relatives to support services

Agencies need to ensure that as many eligible birth relatives as possible are referred to services. It is unlikely that all, or even the majority, of birth relatives are referred or self-refer to services, and there is probably significant potential to increase the numbers of birth relatives referred to adoption support services. The mapping survey showed several models that agencies used to refer eligible relatives for services. These varied in respect of who had responsibility for making the referral and whether there was one or multiple routes into the service (Cossar and Neil, 2009).

The take-up survey showed that there was a significantly higher take up of services amongst birth relatives who self-refer. It is therefore important to ensure that birth relatives are given relevant information about the range of services available at an appropriate time. Social workers in the local authority are the people who know birth relatives, and know who is eligible to receive services, and so they have a vital role in ensuring that birth relatives know what help is available to them. However, relying on birth relatives to self-refer places a lot of responsibility on a vulnerable group who may not trust professionals.

Models which rely on the child's social worker to refer have the advantage that the social worker is intimately involved with the family and in a good position to make a timely referral, given their ongoing knowledge of adoption planning. However, such a system relies on the worker's knowledge and inclination as to whether to make a referral. Many service providers in the mapping survey commented on the difficulties in reliably receiving referrals from child and family social workers, attributing this to high staff turnover, caseload priorities and lack of adoption experience (Sellick, 2007). One way to increase the priority given to birth relative support by child care social workers would be for the adoption panel to routinely inquire whether the birth relatives had been referred for support at the time that the panel considers whether adoption is in the best interests of the child.

Few people in the take-up survey were being referred by other professionals. Accepting referrals from a range of professionals may increase the chances of a timely referral from a worker whom the birth relative trusts. However, this increases the onus on adoption support services to provide training and up-to-date information about their services to numerous professionals. The more universal the service, the less likely the professional is to encounter adoption issues regularly. More specialist services such as substance misuse and mental health may encounter adoption more regularly and these services need to work closely with adoption support services to increase workers' awareness of adoption-related issues and of available support services. Professionals involved specifically with adoption, such as solicitors representing the parent, are in a good position to refer birth relatives, although research by After Adoption (2007) found that many did not see it as part of their role.

It could be argued that there is no point in referring birth relatives who do not want to use the service. However, there may be benefits in doing so: some birth relatives who are initially reluctant to use services may wish to do so at a later stage. If they have the phone number or other details of an agency that can help them, or if they remember a positive contact in the past, they may be more likely to access services in the future.

It is important that agencies keep records relating the take-up of services to method of referral to inform referral practices in the future. Agencies could collaborate to share best practice. An example of this is a network group meeting regularly facilitated by the St Francis Children's Society in Milton Keynes.

Take-up of services

Low take-up of services was identified as an issue by 90 per cent of respondents in the mapping survey. In some cases, respondents identified that they had problems getting birth relatives to begin to use services, but that once they did so they usually continued and found them beneficial. In addition to problems receiving referrals, practitioners identified two other main factors affecting take-up. Firstly, many relatives were angry and did not trust that any service could be independent or appropriate to their needs. Secondly, many of the birth relatives had protracted difficulties affecting their lives, making them a hard to reach group of service users.

The take-up survey found that 56 per cent of birth relatives referred used at least one session (for the interview sample the figure was 66%). We can see, therefore, that many birth relatives who are referred for support do not use services. The interview data give an insight into the reasons why people did not take up a service. Some relatives claimed not to know about services while others cited factors including difficulties getting to the venue, the timing or type of support not being right for them, their own mental state, and lack of follow-up from the adoption support agency. Of those interviewed who did take up a service, several commented on persistence on the part of the worker, which encouraged them to engage. For most people this was seen as a sign of care and concern, giving them the opportunity to engage when they felt ready, rather than as an unwelcome intrusion. Some birth relatives also mentioned the importance of the initial contact and first impressions of the worker. Our research suggests that incorporating an outreach approach appears to be a successful strategy, a finding also suggested in the field of family support.

It is established that those services incorporating outreach can be effective in engaging families who are considered to be in need but hard-to-reach. Factors associated with successful engagement include effective multi-agency services, experienced and competent staff or volunteers, personalised services, an understanding of the barriers which particular families or family members face in accessing services, local knowledge and the capacity to establish trusting relationships. (DCSF, 2009, p 36)

Types of support

The research did not compare particular models of service and relate them to outcomes. This was largely because we did not identify sufficiently distinct models of service provision. However, it was possible to identify differences in the range and amount of services provided. Interview data identified that birth relatives had a range of needs that varied according to the stage of the adoption process. The following types of support were identified.

Emotional support

A key way that birth relatives received support was through the provision of formal counselling sessions. As well as formal sessions, many birth relatives described informal emotional support provided by their worker, either in between sessions or after formal counselling had finished. Indeed, some birth relatives who found formal counselling unhelpful and even upsetting were able to benefit from the more informal emotional support from the caseworker.

Advice and information

This included information about care proceedings and the adoption process, information about their rights and services available to them. Sometimes relatives were informed of practices that may not have been suggested to them by children's services, such as the possibility that they might meet the adopters.

Assistance with contact and communication with their children

Some birth relatives were provided with support with keeping in contact with their children. This might include support with letter writing, including practical help, explanation of the rules and emotional support in undertaking this difficult task. A number of birth relatives also received support to contribute to life story work for their children, and this might take place some time after the adoption.

Advocacy and liaison

In many cases, this involved a worker liaising with agencies to obtain case-specific information on behalf of the parent or an update on the child's welfare. It might also include helping a birth relative to write to an adoption panel, or accompanying a birth relative to meetings. Several workers had liaised with social services to clarify contact arrangements, or chase missing or late letters. Advocacy in some cases helped the birth relative to contain their anger and thus participate in significant decision-making forums.

Group support

Several birth relatives found group support valuable in reducing isolation and providing the opportunity to discuss feelings and issues with peers who shared similar experiences. These themes are also found in the practice literature (Perl and McSkimming, 1997; Harris and Whyte, 1999; Post Adoption Centre, 2000). Thus, group work may be particularly valuable for birth relatives in counteracting the stigma surrounding compulsory adoption.

The findings of the research give some indication about the relationship between the nature of support services and outcomes. The provision of a number of different types of support activities was related to satisfaction. In particular, emotional support and advice and information were associated with service user satisfaction.

Satisfaction with services: what works for birth relatives?

About three-quarters of birth relatives were extremely positive about the services they had received. Very few birth relatives were negative. The self-reports of the birth relatives who took part in the research strongly endorsed the value of support services to birth relatives. The fact that people *feel* helped should be accepted as an important outcome in its own right. Three key aspects of support services were identified as important: the quality of relationship with the worker; confidentiality and independence; and a proactive and flexible approach.

The quality of the relationship with the worker

The opportunity to have a safe and supportive relationship with support workers in birth relatives support services was highly valued and, in the view of some service users, was a vehicle for constructive change in their lives. In keeping with other research on client satisfaction, birth relatives appreciated workers who conveyed care, were able to empathise and were non-judgemental (Mayer and Timms, 1970; Cree and Davis, 2006; Howe, 1993; 2008; Doel and Best, 2008). A relationship-based service seems particularly appropriate for this group of service users: the birth relatives in our study described problems with relationships throughout their life – with their own parents, with their partners, with their children and with professionals. The adoption process involves being judged inadequate as a parent by a court in a formal adversarial system. It is understandable that birth relatives would find it difficult to trust professionals. It is clear from our interviews with birth relatives that relationship-based work does not necessarily have to be a traditional counselling-type arrangement. There were many people whom we spoke to who were resistant to the idea of *counselling* but yet very much valued emotional support. What birth relatives experienced as emotionally supportive encompassed a wide range of activities on the part of the worker, for example, a phone call at the right time, going to a meeting with someone, sending a card, even practical activities like providing transport. While some birth relatives were very defensive about talking about their own past or failures in their parenting, almost everybody appreciated feeling cared about. As Sudbery (2002) argues, sometimes a social worker 'has to actively reach out and demonstrate helpfulness in a practical way' (Sudbery 2002, p 154). In cases where people resist deep emotional work initially, this may be achieved at a later stage once a trusting relationship is established.

Confidentiality and independence

For most birth relatives, the perceived independence of the support service was highly valued. Most services in this study were provided by independent agencies so we have not been able to develop a systematic comparison between such services and those provided in-house by local authorities. However, the low take-up in the agencies providing in-house support may partly reflect birth relatives' unwillingness to engage with the department that is involved in taking their child. Another explanation is that agencies specialising in adoption support may have developed innovative practices to encourage take-up of services, thus leading to the difference. It is clear that birth relatives appreciate access to an independent worker, as laid out in the National Adoption Standards. Whether the independent worker could be part of another team within the local authority or should come from an independent agency cannot be determined by this study. A few birth relatives were sceptical that agencies were truly independent of social services and were aware of commissioning arrangements and of independent agencies' multiple roles including placing children for adoption. Other birth relatives mentioned that they had formed positive relationships with contact support services that were part of local authority provision.

Flexibility and a proactive approach

Given the complexity and range of birth relative's needs, it is understandable that diversity was appreciated in terms of what, when and how services were delivered. The timing of adoption support services is crucial, as birth relatives have different needs at different stages of the adoption process. This lends support to the conclusion of a CSCI inspection report (2006), which suggested that services work best when there is a choice about how and when they can be accessed. A barrier to helping birth relatives early in the adoption process is that they may not want to acknowledge that adoption is a possible outcome. Support services labelled as adoption support services therefore may erect barriers. One agency (After Adoption) has already addressed this issue by re-branding its service for birth relatives as Birth Ties. In the early stages of the adoption process, people seem particularly to need advice and information about what is essentially a very confusing process. Birth relatives appreciated workers with expertise in adoption who understood the process and could be proactive in liaising with agencies on their behalf. Our statistical analysis revealed significant associations between birth relatives who reported receiving advice and information and emotional support and satisfaction with services.

Flexibility regarding the type of service offered was also important. Some birth relatives found attending a predetermined number of formal counselling sessions useful whilst others appreciated a more open-ended "casework" service in which the worker was free to respond to a range of needs, offering both practical and emotional support as required and being available outside of office hours and outside of the office environment. What appears to be important is that the service offered is needs-led. That some agencies are offering a great deal of flexibility in their service provision is demonstrated by the large variation in cost incurred in supporting different individuals. We also found a relationship between the number of services received and satisfaction with them, such that for every additional service received, the birth relative was twice as likely to judge themselves satisfied with services. It is apparent that birth relatives benefit from a range of services and it is likely that different services will come to the fore at different stages in the adoption process.

The costs and outcomes of support

In our analysis, there was a correspondence between what service agencies reported delivering and what service users said they had received. The average service cost of delivering a service to an individual was £511 a year. One might expect this figure to rise if take up rates were improved, and this average cost, based on 2007 figures, may be an under-estimate.

There was evidence from our statistical analyses that support services were having a positive impact on those people using them. Improvement in mental health was significantly related to resource use and cost, and people who had used services were coping significantly better than those who had not. Given the complex and long-standing nature of problems that birth relatives experience and the relatively short follow-up period in this study, it is encouraging that services costing on average about £500 a year were making measurable differences.

The role of other services

Adult services such as mental health and substance misuse services need to be made aware of the adoption-related needs of their service users. Adoption support workers have a role in signposting birth relatives to specialist services, for example, if they are experiencing depression, the urge to self-harm, or using drink or drugs as a coping strategy. Although the majority of birth relatives in our study had very high levels of psychological distress, only a minority of people had received NHS mental health services. Of those who had, counselling was the most common service offered. In most cases, people did not feel that this counselling had met their needs in relation to problems following from the child's adoption. Increased partnership working between adoption support services and specialist adult services seems advisable. This would help alert adult services to the needs of birth relatives and would also assist adoption support services to develop strategies to engage birth relatives with particular needs (such as learning difficulties or mental health issues). An example of innovative provision includes After Adoption's project working through drug and alcohol services to reach vulnerable young mothers (Camelot Foundation and After Adoption, 2008).

The role of children's services

Although this research primarily studied birth relatives' experiences of services delivered in the independent sector, the findings of the study also have many implications for workers in the statutory sector, and these are discussed below.

The birth relatives' accounts reflect their experience of the adoption process as an unfair, disempowering and confusing process. It is not surprising, then, that negative emotions can be focused on the social workers on the frontline viewed as responsible for removing the child. The challenge for social workers in children's services should not be underestimated. The welfare of the child is the key focus of activity. To maintain practice that is ethical in its treatment of birth parents, workers need to have manageable caseloads, good training and good supervision (Horwath, 2005). However, although it is understandable that social workers may bear the brunt of hostility from birth relatives, it would be a defensive reaction to assume that therefore no lessons about best practice can be gleaned from their accounts. Indeed, most birth relatives could identify at least one social work professional whom they had found helpful. Four themes emerged in the interviews that were important attributes of good child care social work: honesty, openness and integrity; availability, reliability and competence of workers; being informed, involved and consulted about key events; and a sensitive and supportive attitude where the worker recognised the relative's distress.

Birth relatives' accounts suggest that if the adoption process can be handled as fairly and openly as possible, some of the negative impact of adoption could be reduced. Government guidance on working in partnership in child protection describes four approaches to partnership working: providing information, involvement, participation and partner-ship (Department of Health, 1995). The level and degree of partnership will fluctuate at different stages in the child protection process. Providing information is the minimum level and stresses the importance of sharing accurate and comprehensible information with the family and making sure that what is conveyed is understood. Higher levels of partnership range from being present at meetings to being part of decision-making on key issues. Whilst it may be unrealistic and disingenuous to speak of working in partnership in the adoption process, minimum levels of information sharing should be achievable and where workers are open and honest about their concerns and their plans, this is appreciated by birth relatives.

Despite the complexity and longevity of birth relatives' problems, it is the parenting problems that attract the attention of children's services and are the focus of professionals' intervention. The child care social worker may have an intensive working relationship with the parent up until the final hearing in care proceedings. The parent may be the focus of much professional activity and assessment, which then ceases suddenly at the conclusion of proceedings, adding to the birth relative's perception that they no longer matter (see also Charlton *et al*, 1998). An example of good practice is of a child care social worker who called the relative after the conclusion of the hearing – although the birth relative felt hostile, this phone call made her feel that she mattered and influenced her later decision to work with social services for the remainder of the adoption process.

Interview data suggested that many birth relatives experience an acute reaction following the immediate loss of the child, and during this phase, ability to cope is very low. Children's services should recognise that it is often during this crisis period that important decisions are made, such as whether the birth relative can meet the adoptive parents and the level and type of contact post-adoption. The birth relatives' degree of co-operation may be a factor in such decisions, and agencies need to bear in mind that, at the time decisions are made, they may be witnessing birth relatives at their lowest level of co-operation and functioning. Birth relatives may need support to take up these potentially helpful opportunities; they may need to have them presented to them more than once; and in some cases missed opportunities may need to be revisited in the post-placement era.

It is clear that birth relatives need support once the child is placed for adoption. At this point, child care services are still involved with the child. One-third of birth relatives experienced the *contact gap*, a period of uncertainty between their farewell contact with the child and the commencement of post-adoption indirect contact, which could last up to two years. This gap is a missed opportunity in helping the parent to adjust and offer reassurance about the welfare of the child. The introduction of placement orders by the 2002 Act may lead to birth parents with parental responsibility receiving more information during this period, since they retain parental responsibility until the making of the adoption order. Contact plans and arrangements need to be made clear to birth relatives, preferably in writing. If birth parents have not been able to engage constructively in conversations about contact prior to the adoption being finalised, they should have the opportunity to do so at a later stage.

Post-adoption, a number of birth relatives received support from the local authority, especially post-adoption teams and staff managing letterbox contact services. Many spoke positively of the support that they received for contact. This shows that it is possible for birth relatives to work positively with local authorities which were involved in removing their children. Local authorities clearly have a role in conducting the adoption in a fair and open manner and they have an ongoing role after the adoption in managing contact. Support for contact may provide a further opportunity to access wider adoption support for some birth relatives.

The needs of birth fathers

The Equality Act 2006 created a gender equality duty. Local authorities must seek to eliminate discrimination on the grounds of gender and to promote equality of opportunity between men and women. This means that local authorities must be proactive in considering the differing needs of men and women in the development of public services. A recurrent theme across the research concerned the needs of birth fathers and the services provided to them. The service take-up survey showed that in the interview sample, more mothers used services regularly than did fathers, the majority of whom had only had a brief service.

Our findings suggest that the impact of adoption on both fathers and grandparents is just as great as it is on birth mothers. This dispels any myth that these other relatives are not as badly affected by the loss of the child to adoption as birth mothers. On both the BSI mental health measure and the coping with adoption scale, the data suggested that birth fathers may be less likely to improve over time in these aspects of functioning compared to birth mothers. Researchers studying spousal bereavement argue that men have more difficulties adjusting to the loss of a spouse than women, proposing that this is due to the greater availability of other sources of support for women compared to men (Strobe and Strobe, 1993), and the same reasoning may be true of men's adjustment to adoption-related loss.

There is clearly a need for further research to consider the needs of birth fathers. Compared to birth mothers, birth fathers were less likely to be referred for support and less likely to take up support – why are so few fathers being referred? Why are fathers reluctant to use services?

There is scant research on the support needs of fathers in compulsory adoption although there is some relevant research in the child protection field. Scourfield conducted ethnographic research in a child protection team looking at the construction of gender within the office. He found that men were viewed pejoratively as 'a threat, as no use, as irrelevant and as absent' (2009, p 443). It was assumed that women were ultimately responsible for children. If such attitudes are widespread amongst social care workers, a predominantly female workforce, then this may in part explain the difference in referral rates to adoption support for men and women. If fathers are less likely than mothers to be involved in the child care social work processes leading up to adoption, they may be less likely to be referred on for support. Page *et al* (2008) interviewed managers involved in safeguarding children on engaging fathers in family services. Interviewees felt that attempts to engage biological fathers were high in the safeguarding field, partly because of court requirements to consider different members of the family as potential carers for children. Barriers to engagement raised by managers included lack of time to pursue non-resident fathers who did not have a great deal of involvement with their children; lack of male social workers; and lack of training for social workers in dealing with aggressive fathers. They raised the need for a better evidence base to guide practice with fathers of children at risk. The report makes general recommendations about engaging fathers in family services. These include: routinely monitoring engagement of fathers; ensuring that services appeal to fathers' interests; use of outreach; ensuring communications include positive images of fathers; and recruiting more male staff to the workforce. These recommendations could also apply to adoption support services.

There needs to be more research on the needs of fathers whose children have been adopted to ensure that support services are providing the right help. Services specifically tailored to men's needs may need to be offered. For example, Clapton (2007) argues that birth fathers may need to be offered support that is practical or action-focused rather than emotion-focused. This would fit with other research on fathers and family support services, which suggests that men are less comfortable than women in identifying problems and seeking help with them, and they may be less able to talk about their feelings than women (O'Brien, 2004).

Links between the welfare of birth relatives and the welfare of adopted children

This research has studied compulsory adoption from the point of view of birth parents and grandparents. It has illuminated the psychological challenges that this experience presents to birth relatives. We have seen that the loss of the child is at the heart of the experience, a loss that is involuntary, stigmatising and ambiguous. This leaves birth relatives needing to surmount a range of issues connected to, but beyond, the loss of the child.

The loss challenges a birth relative's sense of identity. A sense of self as an adequate parent or grandparent is difficult to sustain in the face of legal proceedings that conclude otherwise. The stigma attached to this type of loss has a profound impact on both people's internal world, and their ability to access external support. After adoption, birth relatives must consider who they are in relation to their child or grandchild. Almost everyone we spoke to continued to feel a profound sense of connection to the child, but in the face of legal and physical separation, there were few opportunities to express this connection or understand if or how their child felt connected to them. The nature of being a parent or grandparent was radically altered by the adoption, requiring birth relatives to consider what type of a parent or grandparent they could be to a child who, in most cases, they could not see, touch, hug, or communicate directly with. The child now had other people putting them to bed, taking them to school, and possessing the title of mummy or daddy. All of these issues require birth relatives to undergo a radical re-evaluation of self.

Coping with the knowledge of the child's continued existence, but having very limited (and in some cases no) information about the detail of his or her life and development, made the loss ambiguous: although physically absent, psychologically the child remained strongly present (Fravel et al, 2000). The work of Henney et al (2004) found that different types of openness in adoption present different satisfactions and problems to birth mothers. Where there was little or no contact with the child, worries about his or her well-being were high. In contrast, mothers who had ongoing direct contact mainly felt more happy about the outcomes of adoption of their child but at the same time they felt challenged in understanding their role and relationship with the adoptive family: the doubt about the child's welfare was reduced through ongoing contact, but the ambiguity of who birth parents were in relation to the child was increased.

In addition to dealing with difficult feelings of grief, anger, shame and guilt, birth relatives have to find a way to go on with their lives after adoption, and adapt to the changes in role and identity that adoption has brought about. As has been argued in relation to bereavement (Bowlby, 1980; Parkes, 2001), coping with loss requires re-organisation not just psychologically but in terms of day-to-day living. Coping with bereavement involves the dual processes of loss orientation and restoration orientation (Stroebe and Schut, 1999); the latter involves coping with secondary losses, such as changes in role and identity. Too much focus on loss orientation may lead to chronic grief. On the other hand, if dealing with the loss is constantly avoided and if there is a focus on carrying on as normal, this may lead to grief that is suppressed or denied. Hence coping successfully with the stresses of bereavement necessitates both loss orientation and restoration orientation. This theory would suggest therefore that support for birth relatives needs to be both emotion-focused and focused on coping with change and constructing a different identity in terms of being a parent, and a different way of living.

Meeting the individual needs of birth relatives is important in its own right but if further justification for providing birth relative support is required, then it is worth considering the impact of these support services beyond the individual birth relative. It is now widely recognised that, although adoption constitutes a complete legal transfer of the child from one family into another, psychologically the child remains connected to his or her birth family, and the birth and adoptive family become connected to each other in the adoption kinship network (Reitz and Watson, 1992). These psychological connections come to life in post-adoption contact, and the current reality is that most adopted children will have a plan for some form of contact with birth relatives. Contact is most likely to be beneficial for the adopted child when both his or her birth parents (or other relatives) and adoptive parents recognise the child's connection to both families (Beek and Schofield, 2004) and where the adults can understand and support each other in their differing roles (Grotevant, 2009; Neil, 2009). Post-adoption contact is more than a letter or a meeting: it is about relationships. Even when the contact constitutes a minimal exchange of written information, in writing and receiving this information, birth relatives, adoptive parents, and adopted children (assuming they are involved) must relate to the other person in their own mind: What do they want to know? How will they interpret what is written? What do I think of them? What do they think of me?

Within the adoption kinship network, each person brings four elements: developmental history, expectations about relationships, expectations about the adoption, and relationship skills (Grotevant, 2009) and each of these four elements is likely to have an effect on how the network as a whole operates. This means that post-adoption contact is both dynamic (it is likely to change over time) and transactional (how one person behaves, thinks, or feels is likely to have an impact on how other people behave, think and feel) (Neil and Howe, 2004). For example, when birth relatives show acceptance of the child's place in the adoptive family, this may reassure adopters about their position as parents, and allow children to move on and form new relationships. On the other hand, if birth relatives are dismissive of adoptive parents, or expect children to continue to show them primary loyalty, this can make adoptive parents anxious and leave children feeling angry, guilty, or unable to settle. If birth relatives are unable to maintain planned contact over time, this can also have an impact on children and adoptive parents, possibly bringing about a sense of disappointment or feelings of rejection, and leaving the child's actual and future questions unanswered. Good quality post-adoption contact can benefit adopted children, but failed or poor quality contact can pose risks. In many cases, maximising benefits and minimising risks will require post-adoption contact to be supported. Support specifically for birth parents is an important consideration but one that workers may sometimes overlook (Neil, 2007b).

Although most adoptions today include a plan for openness, in many cases these arrangements may never become firmly established. For example, Neil (2004) found that six years post-placement, 50 per cent of planned letterbox contact arrangements had either stopped entirely or did not include any response from birth relatives. Curiosity about the birth family appears to be natural for adopted children and this curiosity is fuelled when children have information gaps (Wrobel and Dillon, 2009). Although adoption is now more open, adopted children are still likely to have information gaps in the future, either because contact has failed or is of poor quality, or because certain birth relatives are not involved in the arrangements. So it is reasonable to predict that some of today's children adopted from care will go looking for information about their birth relatives at some point in the future. What will they encounter? The adjustment of birth relatives to the adoption may be relevant to the adopted person in the future if he or she then seeks some contact with their birth family members. For example, in a study of post-reunion relationships between birth mothers and their now adult adopted children (Kelly, 2009), these relationships worked more successfully when birth mothers showed an acceptance that they could never be the kind of mother they might wish to be to their child. Instead, it was helpful when birth mothers recognised that they may develop a friendship with their adopted child but they could not replace the child's adoptive mother.

The current research has illustrated the immensely difficult feelings of birth relatives about losing their children in compulsory adoption, and the difficult and complex lives of birth relatives. If birth relatives remain stuck in the same emotional space they were thrust into in the aftermath of the adoption, this is very likely to affect any future contact or relation-ship with the adopted person. How will it feel for the adopted person to hear their birth relatives' perspective of how unfairly they were treated, how blighted their life has been, how angry they feel? What might it be like for the adopted person to meet with the birth parent who hopes and expects to take up where they left off many years ago as "mum" or "dad"? Adopted children, especially those who remember and continue to be affected by histories of abuse and neglect, may be helped if their birth family members can see and acknowledge the child's feelings, experience and perspective, and support them in working through difficult feelings.

In short, whether or not post-adoption contact occurs, the fate of birth relatives is not and cannot be entirely divorced from the fate of the adopted child. If birth relatives receive support which helps them to cope with adoption, to accept their child's other family, to re-orientate their own lives, and to maintain a supportive participation in contact, this is likely to benefit both adopted children and adoptive parents either immediately or in the future. In addition, many birth parents are likely to go on to have other children. Most people in our interview sample had more than one child, but very few people had been able to retain their parenting role with any of their children. Many people expressed the desire to have future children, and some had already done so. Unsuccessful management of the impact of the loss of previous children is likely to affect the parenting of future children. Several of the birth relatives who took part in our study, and many of those who were members of our consultancy groups, identified as a gap in provision services that would help the birth parents to keep their subsequent children.

There was evidence from this research that adoption support services were able to help birth relatives to deal with many of the issues described above. The type of service people most commonly reported receiving was emotional support. It is not difficult to understand why this was helpful to birth relatives in dealing with their sense of self, and their feelings and expectations about others. Most birth relatives had difficult experiences of relationships, and as Howe explains, 'If poor relationships are where things emotionally go wrong then healthy relationships are where things can be put right' (2008, p 161). The interventions employed to help birth relatives were not, in the most part, specialist and therapeutic models requiring a high level of worker training. They constituted what many people would recognise as social casework. They were not expensive when compared to other health and social care costs (Curtis, 2007) and compared to the cost of adoption support for adoptive families (Selwyn et al, 2004), yet service user satisfaction was very high, and some improvements in adjustment were evident.

There was a high level of correspondence between professionals' views of birth relatives' support needs (as expressed in our mapping study) and birth relatives' views of their own needs, suggesting there is already a great deal of professional expertise in the field of birth parent support. In the main part, services seemed well conceived and delivered. Nevertheless, suggestions for the development of services in the future can be considered. On the basis of this research, we would suggest that services could evolve in ways that more specifically address a range of psychological tasks that challenge birth relatives. Services already seem well developed in terms of helping people cope with loss, and with negotiating the adoption process. There may be room to develop dimensions that have a more specific focus on aspects of adjustment that are relevant to the child, such as accepting dual connection, participating positively in contact, managing the "telling" of the adoption story (both to self and to others), and on re-orientating a life post-adoption.

Implications for practice

This final section of the book brings together implications for practice suggested by this research. In identifying these, we have drawn on the data from this study, the contributions of practitioners who participated in the mapping stage of the study, the ideas of our birth relative consultancy groups, and contributions made by members of the birth relative support services network group, facilitated by the St Francis' Children's Society.

Suggestions for birth relative support service providers

Engaging birth relatives in using services: service providers could consider a range of outreach methods, including:

- a phone line to provide out of hours support;
- drop-in sessions and "duty" services so birth relatives can access support outside of scheduled appointments;
- persistence in following up referrals by phone, text messaging, home visiting;
- offer the services at an agency base and at other venues including birth relatives' homes and in prisons;
- flexibility about birth relatives leaving and returning to services;
- liaison with other service providers likely to be in contact with birth relatives to publicise services on offer and raise awareness of the impact of adoption on birth relatives;
- liaison with other service providers to seek advice about appropriate methods of working with birth relatives who have special

needs (e.g. related to disability, mental health, literacy, language or culture);

- having a physical presence in other service locations (for example, regular "surgery" sessions at a drug and alcohol advisory service);
- publicising services widely through a range of specialist and community networks;
- considering how services are marketed to birth relatives to avoid creating unnecessary barriers (for example, implications that services are only for "after" adoption, avoiding describing workers as social workers, etc) and to emphasise the range of services that are available. The involvement of birth relatives in the design of marketing materials could be helpful;
- monitoring sources of referral and uptake to learn what works;
- sharing ideas and expertise with other birth relative support providers, for example, via consortia or network groups;
- involving service users in the design, delivery and evaluation of services;
- offering specialist services where the needs of the local population suggest this (for example, to meet the needs of birth relatives of minority ethnicity);
- developing father involvement strategies. This may include employing male workers and offering services specifically targeted at fathers;

Providing a broad range of services appropriate to individual need and to the different stages of adoption. In addition to the five types of service identified in the study, service providers could consider:

- the use of other birth relatives as peer support workers/volunteers;
- online information and support via websites and discussion groups;
- interventions to help birth relatives manage the process of under-standing and telling their story of the adoption, for example, life story work with birth relatives, and help to anticipate and deal with the reactions of other people to the adoption (this could include rehearsing or role-playing how to respond in certain situations);

- use of the creative arts to help express feelings;
- social activities (to reduce isolation);
- help and advice with activities birth relatives could undertake to help them restore/re-orientate their lives after adoption, for example, hobbies, interests, education, voluntary work;
- helping birth relatives to understand the needs of their child as an adopted person and the needs of adoptive families (for example, raising awareness of how adopted people feel by using video material, or visits to a birth parent group by an adopted person or adoptive parent);
- liaising with children's services to enable the participation of birth relatives in life story work or letters for later life for the child (birth relative support workers may be able to undertake some of this work with birth relatives);
- providing information about the contact register and birth relative intermediary services;
- providing services focused on helping birth parents who are planning to have more children, or who are parenting subsequent children;

Suggestions for local authority children's services

Local authorities can do much to help birth relatives by following principles of partnership working with birth parents before adoption. Suggestions specific to partnership working in adoption could include:

- providing a simple fact sheet about the adoption process containing key phone numbers for sources of support;
- meetings with adoptive parents – unless risk assessment indicates otherwise, facilitate meetings between birth relatives (including where relevant fathers and other relatives) and the adoptive parents, and prepare and support birth relatives to participate in these. If these meetings cannot happen when first offered, attempts to arrange the meeting at a later date, possibly after adoption, could be made;
- involve birth relatives in planning for post-adoption contact and ensure that birth relatives have clear explanations of when and how

post-adoption contact will happen;

- address the issue of the contact gap – ensure there is a planned transition from when direct contact ceases through to when post-adoption contact begins (for example, information about the child's progress could be sent to birth relatives following children's reviews);
- final direct contact with the child – ensure that birth relatives have adequate preparation and support for these meetings, where necessary, involving birth relative support workers;
- provide birth relatives with non-identifying information about adoptive parents;
- let parents know, in writing, when children have been placed and adopted;
- inviting birth relatives to the "should be placed for adoption recommendation" adoption panel;
- including a birth relative as a member of the adoption panel;
- where birth relatives are working with independent support workers, keep these workers informed of key stages and events so they can remind and support birth relatives;

Increasing the uptake of birth relative support services. Local authorities could consider:

- instituting systems to ensure that all birth relatives are referred to service providers, for example, via independent reviewing officers or adoption panels;
- consider the needs of all involved birth relatives including fathers, grandparents and siblings;
- monitor referral and uptake information;
- where services are provided predominantly in-house, recognise that, for some birth relatives, no matter how good the service, they will refuse to work with the local authority. In such cases, services from another agency or independent worker could be spot purchased;
- when contracting with independent agencies, allow for flexibility over when and for how long services can be accessed and by which

birth relatives (for example, to meet the needs of birth relatives who come back for help some time after the adoption).

Implications for professionals in other agencies

Professionals working within other services who are likely to encounter birth relatives (for example, drug and alcohol workers, mental health workers, learning disability workers, the prison and probation services) have an important role to play in recognising the adoption-related needs of their service users and referring people to adoption support services. Professionals in these teams could consider:

- routinely asking service users whether they have children they are no longer parenting, and recognising the impact of the loss of children to adoption on people;
- referring to, encouraging and supporting birth relatives in using adoption support services;
- working in partnership with birth relatives support providers, for example, to jointly deliver services (e.g. a group for birth parents run within a mental health day service).

References

After Adoption (2007) *Moving From the Sidelines: A Study of the provision of independent support in Wales for the birth parents and relatives of children in the adoption process*, Cardiff: After Adoption

After Adoption (2008) *After Adoption: Specialist interventions with young birth mothers*, Merseyside: After Adoption

Aldgate J. (1980) 'Identification of factors influencing children's length of stay in care', in Triseliotis J. (ed.) *New Developments in Adoption and Fostering*, London: Routledge

Ball C. (2005) 'The Adoption and Children Act 2002: A critical examination', *Adoption & Fostering*, 29:2, pp 6–17

Beek M. and Schofield G. (2004) 'Promoting security and managing risk: contact in long-term foster care', in Neil E. and Howe D. (eds), *Contact in Adoption and Permanent Foster Care: Research, theory and practice*, London: BAAF

Berry M., Cavazos Dylla D. J., Barth R. P. and Needell B. (1998) 'The role of open adoption in the adjustment of adopted children and their families', *Children and Youth Services Review*, 1–2, pp 151–171

Bouchier P., Lambert L. and Triseliotis J. (1991) *Parting with a Child for Adoption: The mother's perspective*, London: BAAF

Bowlby J. (1980) *Attachment and Loss: Volume 3 – Loss, sadness and depression*, London: Penguin

Brammer A. (2003) *Social Work Law*, Harlow: Longman

Brodzinsky D. (2005) 'Reconceptualizing openness in adoption: implications for theory, research and practice', in Brodzinsky D. and Palacios J. (eds.), *Psychological Issues in Adoption: Research and practice*, New York: Greenwood, pp 145–166

Byford S. and Sefton T. (2003) 'Economic evaluation of complex health and social care interventions', *National Institute Economic Review*, 186, pp 98–108

Camelot Foundation and After Adoption (2008) *Transforming Lives: Independent adoption support of birth parents with addiction difficulties*, Manchester: After Adoption

Charlton L., Crank. M., Kansara K. and Oliver C. (1998) *Still Screaming: Birth parents compulsorily separated from their children*, Manchester: After Adoption

Christian C. L., McRoy R. G., Grotevant H. D. and Bryant C. M. (1997) 'The grief resolution of birth mothers in confidential, time-limited mediated, ongoing mediated and fully disclosed adoptions', *Adoption Quarterly*, 1:2, pp 35–58

Cicchini M. (1993) *The Development of Responsibility: The experience of birth fathers in adoption*, West Australia: Adoption Research and Counselling Service

Clapton G. (2003) 'Birth fathers and their adoption experiences', London: Jessica Kingsley Publishers

Clapton G. (2007) 'The experiences and needs of birth fathers in adoption: what we know now and some practice implications', *Practice*, 19, pp 61–71

Condon J. T. (1986) 'Psychological disability in women who relinquish a baby for adoption', *Medical Journal of Australia*, 144, pp 117–119

Cossar J. and Neil E. (2009) 'Supporting the birth relatives of adopted children: how accessible are services?', *The British Journal of Social Work*, Advance access, published on May 31 2009, DOI: 10.1093/bjsw/bcp061

Cree V. E. and Davis A. (2006) *Social Work: Voices from the inside*, New York: Routledge

CSCI (Commission for Social Care Inspection) (2006) *Adoption: Messages from inspections of adoption agencies*, available at: www.csci.org.uk/PDF/adoption_messages_2_[2].pdf, accessed 10/10/08

Curtis L. (2007) *The Unit Costs of Health and Social Care*, Canterbury: Personal Social Services Research Unit

Cushman L. F., Kalmuss D. and Brickner Namerow P. (1997) 'Openness in adoption: experiences and psychological outcomes among birth mothers', *Marriage and Family Review*, 25, pp 7–18

Department of Health (1995) *The Challenge of Partnership in Child Protection: Practice guide*, London: HMSO

Department of Health (2001) *National Adoption Standards for England*, London: DOH

Department of Health and Welsh Assembly Government (2003) *Adoption: National Minimum Standards*, London: The Stationary Office

Department of Children, Schools and Families (2009) *Outreach to Children and Families: A scoping study*, Research report DCSF-RR116, London: DCSF

Derogatis L. R. (1993) *BSI: Brief Symptom Inventory: Administration, scoring and procedures manual*, Minneapolis: National Computer Systems, Inc

Deykin E. Y., Campbell L. and Patti P. (1984) 'The post-adoption experience of surrendering parents', *American Journal of Orthopsychiatry*, 54, pp 271–280

Deykin E. Y., Patti P. and Ryan J. (1988) 'Fathers of adopted children: a study of the impact of surrender on birth fathers', *American Journal of Orthopsychiatry*, 58, pp 240–248

Doel M. and Best L. (2008) *Experiencing Social Work: Learning from service users*, London: Sage

Doka K. J. (2002) (ed.) *Disenfranchised Grief: Recognizing hidden sorrow*, Lexington, MA: Lexington Books

Etter J. (1993) 'Levels of co-operation and satisfaction in 56 open adoptions', *Child Welfare*, 72, pp 257–267

Festinger T. (1986) *Necessary Risk: A study of adoptions and disrupted adoptive placements*, Washington DC: The Child Welfare League of America

Fravel D. L., McRoy R. G. and Grotevant H. D. (2000) 'Birth mother perceptions of the psychologically present adopted child: adoption openness and boundary ambiguity', *Family Relations*, 49, pp 425–33

Freeman P. and Hunt J. (1998) *Parental Perspectives on Care Proceedings*, London: The Stationary Office

Goffman E. (1963) *Stigma: Notes on the management of a spoiled identity*, Englewood Cliffs, NJ: Prentice-Hall

Grotevant H. D. (2009) 'Emotional distance regulation over the life course in adoptive kinship networks', in Wrobel G and Neil E (eds) *International Advances in Adoption Research for Practice*, Chichester: Wiley

Grotevant H. D., Ross N. M., Marcel M. A. and McRoy R. G. (1999) 'Adaptive behaviour in adopted children: predictors from early risk, collaboration in relationships within the adoptive kinship network, and openness arrangements', *Journal of Adolescent Research*, 14:2, pp 231–247

Handley B., Bradburn J., Barnes M., Evans C., Goodare H., Kelson M., Kent A., Oliver S., Thomas S. and Wallcraft J. (2003) *Involving the Public in NHS, Public Health, and Social Care Research: Briefing notes for researchers* (second edition), Eastleigh: INVOLVE

Harris F. and Whyte N. (1999) 'Support for birth mothers in a group setting', *Adoption & Fostering*, 23:4, pp 41–48

Harris P. (2005) 'Family is family . . . it does affect everybody in the family: black birth relatives and adoption support', *Adoption & Fostering*, 29:2, pp 66–74

Henney S. M., Ayers-Lopez S., McRoy R. G. and Grotevant H. D. (2004) 'A longitudinal perspective on changes in adoption openness: the birth mother story', in Neil E. and Howe D. (eds), *Contact in Adoption and Permanent Foster Care*, London: BAAF, pp 26–45

Henney S. M., Ayers-Lopez S., McRoy G. and Grotevant H. D. (2007) 'Evolution and resolution: birth mothers' experience of grief and loss at different levels of adoption openness', *Journal of Social and Personal Relationships*, 24, pp 875–889

Horwath J. (2005) 'Identifying and assessing cases of child neglect: learning from the Irish Experience', *Child and Family Social Work*, 10:2, pp 99–110

Howe D. (1993) *On Being a Client: Understanding the process of counselling and psychotherapy*, London: Sage

Howe D. (2008) *The Emotionally Intelligent Social Worker*, Basingstoke: Palgrave Macmillan

Howe D., Sawbridge P. and Hinings D. (1992) *Half a Million Women: Mothers who lose their children by adoption*, London: Penguin

Hughes D. (1997) *What can a Counsellor do? A personal account of counselling by a mother who parted with her child for adoption*, London: Post Adoption Centre

Iwanek M. (1987) *A Study of Open Adoption Placements*, 14 Emerson Street, Petone, New Zealand (unpublished)

Jackson J. (2000) 'Developing a post-adoption groupwork service for non-consenting birth mothers', *Adoption & Fostering*, 24:4, pp 32–39

Jenkins S. and Norman E. (1972) *Filial Deprivation and Foster Care*, New York: Columbia University Press

Kelly R. (2009) 'Emerging voices-reflections on adoption from the birth mother's perspective', in Wrobel G. and Neil E. (eds) *International Advances in Adoption Research for Practice*, Chichester: Wiley

Lindley B. (1994) *Families in Court: A qualitative study of families' experiences of the court process in care and supervision proceedings under the Children Act 1989*, London: Family Rights Group

Logan J. (1996) 'Birth mothers and their mental health: unchartered territory', *British Journal of Social Work*, 26, pp 609–625

Logan J. (1999) 'Exchanging information post adoption: views of adoptive parents and birth parents', *Adoption & Fostering*, 23:3, pp 27–37

Lowe N., Murch M., Borkowski M., Weaver A., Beckford V. and Thomas C. (1999) *Supporting Adoption: Reframing the Approach*, London: BAAF

Mason K. and Selman P. (1997) 'Birth parents' experiences of contested adoptions', *Adoption & Fostering*, 21:1, pp 21–28

Masson J., Harrison C. and Pavlovic A. (1997) *Working with Children and 'Lost' Parents: Putting partnership into practice*, York: York Publishing Ltd

Mayer J. E. and Timms N. (1970) *The Client Speaks: Working class impressions of casework*, London: Routledge and Kegan Paul

Millham S., Bullock R., Hosie K. and Haak M. (1986) *Lost In Care*, Aldershot: Gower

Murch M., Lowe N., Borkowski M., Copner R. and Griew K. (1993) *Pathways to Adoption*, London: HMSO

Neil E. (2000) 'The reasons why young children are placed for adoption: findings from a recently placed sample and implications for future identity issues', *Child and Family Social Work*, 4:6, pp 303–316

Neil E. (2002a) 'Contact after adoption: the role of agencies in making and supporting plans', *Adoption & Fostering*, 26:1, pp 25–38

Neil E. (2002b) 'Managing face-to-face contact for young adopted children', in Argent H. (ed) *Staying Connected: Managing Contact Arrangements In Adoption*, London: BAAF

Neil E. (2003) 'Accepting the reality of adoption: birth relative's experiences of face-to-face contact', *Adoption & Fostering*, 27:2, pp 32–43

Neil E. (2004) 'The 'Contact after Adoption' study: indirect contact and adoptive parents' communication about adoption', in Neil E. and Howe D. (eds) *Contact in Adoption and Permanent Foster Care: Research, theory and practice*, London: BAAF

Neil E. (2007a) 'Coming to terms with the loss of a child: the feelings of birth parents and grandparents about adoption and post-adoption contact', *Adoption Quarterly*, 10:1, pp 1–23

Neil E. (2007b) 'Supporting post-adoption contact for children adopted from care: a study of social workers' attitudes', *Adoption Quarterly*, 10:2/3, pp 3–28

Neil E. (2009) 'The corresponding experiences of adoptive parents and birth relatives in open adoptions', in Wrobel B. and Neil E. (eds) *International Advances in Adoption Research for Practice*, Chichester: Wiley

Neil E., Beek M. and Schofield G. (2003) 'Thinking about and managing contact in permanent placements: the differences and similarities between adoptive parents and foster carers', *Journal of Clinical Child Psychology and Psychiatry*, 8:3, pp 401–418

Neil E., Cossar J., Jones C., Lorgelly P. and Young J. (2010) 'Supporting post-adoption in complex cases: final report to the DCSF', Norwich: UEA

Neil E. and Howe D. (2004) 'Conclusions: a transactional model for thinking about contact', in Neil E. and Howe D. (eds), *Contact in Adoption and Permanent Foster Care: Research, theory and practice*, London: BAAF, pp 224–254

O'Brien M. (2004) *Fathers and Family Support: Promoting involvement and evaluating impact*, London: National Family and Parenting Institute

O'Neill C. (2003) 'The simplicity and complexity of support', in Argent H. (ed.) *Models of Adoption Support: What works and what doesn't*, London: BAAF

Page J., Whittling G. and Mclean C. (2008) *A Review of how Fathers can be Better Recognised and Supported through DCSF Policy*, DCSF research report DCSF-RR040, Nottingham: DCSF Publications

Parker R. (1999) *Adoption Now: Messages from research*, London: The Stationary Office

Parkes C. M. (1971) 'Psycho-social transitions: a field for study', *Social Science & Medicine*, 5:1, pp 101–115

Parkes C. M. (2001) *Bereavement: Studies of grief in adult life* (third edition), Philadelphia, PA: Taylor and Francis

Perl L. and McSkimming J. (1997) 'No longer ashamed and alone: the experience of a birth mother's weekend group', *Australian Social Work*, 50:1, pp 45–49

Post-Adoption Centre (2000) *Thoughts on Adoption by Birth Mothers in Contested Adoptions*, London: Post Adoption Centre

Powell S. and Warren J. (1997) *The Easy Way Out? Birth Mothers: The Hidden Side of Adoption*, London: Minerva Press

Reitz M. and Watson K. W. (1992) *Adoption and the Family System*, New York, NY: The Guilford Press

Rockel J. and Ryburn M. (1988) *Adoption Today: Change and Choice in New Zealand*, Auckland: Heinemann/Reed

Rowe J., Cain H., Hundleby M. and Keane A. (1984) *Long-Term Foster Care*, London: Batsford

Rushton A. and Dance C. (2002) *Adoption Support Services for Families in Difficulty: A literature review and UK survey*, London: BAAF

Ryburn M. (1994) 'Contact after contested adoptions', *Adoption & Fostering*, 18:4, pp 30–37

Sass D. A. and Henderson D. B. (2002) 'Adoptees' and birth parents' therapeutic experiences related to adoption', *Adoption Quarterly*, 6:1, pp 25–32

Scourfield J. (2009) 'The challenge of engaging fathers in the child protection process', *Critical Social Policy* 26:2, pp 440–449

Sellick C. (2007) 'An examination of adoption support services for birth relatives and for post-adoption contact in England and Wales', *Adoption & Fostering*, 31:4, pp 17–26

Sellick C., Neil E., Lorgelly P., Healey N. and Young J. (2006) *Supporting the Birth Relatives of Adopted Children and Supporting Post-Adoption Contact in Complex Cases: A study of service provision, costs and outcomes – Stage one report to Department for Education and Skills – Service mapping*, Norwich: Centre for Research on the Child and Family, University of East Anglia

Selwyn J., Quinton D., Harris P., Wijedasa D., Nawaz S. and Wood M. (2010) *Pathways to Permanence for Black, Asian and Mixed Ethnicity Children*, London: BAAF

Selwyn J., Sempik J., Thurston P. and Wijedasa D. (2009) *Adoption and the Interagency Fee*, Department for Children, Schools and Families Research Briefing, DCSF-RB149

Selwyn J. T., Sturgess W. A., Quinton D. L. and Baxter C. (2004) 'Costs of adoption', in Curtis L. and Netten A. (eds) *Unit Costs of Health and Social Care 2004*, Canterbury: pp 11–17

Smith C. and Logan J. (2004) *After Adoption: Direct contact and relationships*, London: Routledge

Strobe W. and Strobe M. (1993) 'Determinants of adjustment to bereavement in younger widows and widowers', in Strobe M., Strobe W. and Hansson R. (eds) *Handbook of Bereavement: Theory research and intervention*, Cambridge: Cambridge University Press

Stroebe M. and Schut H. (1999) 'The dual process model of coping with bereavement: rationale and description', *Death Studies*, 23:3, pp 197–224

Sudbery J. (2002) 'Key features of therapeutic social work: the use of relationship', *Journal of Social Work Practice*, 16:2, pp 149–162

Thorpe R. (1980) 'The experiences of children and parents living apart: implications and guidelines for practice', in Triseliotis J. (ed.) *New Developments in Adoption and Fostering*, London: Routledge and Kegan Paul

Tingle N. (1994) 'A view of wider family perspectives in contested adoptions', in Ryburn M. (ed.) *Contested Adoptions: Research, law, policy and practice*, Aldershot: Arena

Tingle N. (1995) 'Grandparents speak', in Argent H. (ed.) *See You Soon: Contact with children looked after by local authorities*, London: BAAF

Triseliotis J. (1980) 'Growing up in foster care and after', in Triseliotis J. (ed.) *New Developments in Adoption and Fostering*, London: Routledge and Kegan Paul

Triseliotis J., Shireman J. and Hundleby M. (1997) *Adoption: Theory, Policy and Practice*, London: Cassell

Wells S. (1994) *Within Me, Without Me, Adoption: An open and shut case?* London: Scarlet Press

Winkler R. and Van Keppel M. (1984) *Relinquishing Mothers in Adoption: Their long term adjustment*, Melbourne: Institute of Family Studies

Wrobel G. and Dillon K. (2009) 'Adopted adolescents: who and what are they curious about?', in Wrobel G. and Neil E. (eds) (2009) *International Advances in Adoption Research for Practice*, Chichester: Wiley

Young J. and Neil E. (2004) 'The 'Contact after Adoption' study: the perspective of birth relatives after non-voluntary adoption', in Neil E. and Howe D. (eds.) *Contact in Adoption and Permanent Foster Care: Research, theory and practice*, London: BAAF, pp 85–104

Index

Compiled by Elisabeth Pickard

Please note: unless specified, contact refers to post-adoption contact; adoption to compulsory adoption

alcohol misuse 18, 72–3
anger
    at child's removal 87
    contact letters and 97
    post-adoption 20, 162
    towards LA 34
anxiety
    about child's welfare 87,
        155–7
    post-adoption mental health
        169, 171
Appeal Court, on post-adoption
    contact 12–13
ASAs *see* adoption support
    agencies (ASAs)
availability, of social workers
    90–1

B
bereavement 74, 75, 85–6
betrayal, feelings of 89
birth families
    problems in 71–6
    relationships 72, 75, 139–41
    support network 131
    support service referral by
        63–5
birth fathers
    BSI scores post-adoption
        172–3
    feelings, in relinquishment 17
    interviews with 68–70
    parental responsibility 11
    service take-up 3, 65–6, 102
    support information needs 36,
        132
    support needs 209–10

birth mothers
    BSI scores post-adoption
        172–3
    experiences in adoptions
        17–20, 22–3
    feelings
        in adoptions 17–20
        in relinquishment 14–17
    interviews with 68–70
    service take-up 3, 65–6,
        102
    social workers' views on
        38–9
    views on social workers 21
birth parents
    Adoption and Children Act
        (2002) on support 84
    consultation, in adoptive
        placement 92–4
    impact of child's adoption
        165–6
        coping with 5, 157–64
    interviews with 68–70
    own childhood adversity 73,
        75, 76, 80
birth relatives
    in adoption process 17–20
    experiences 3–7, 14–28
    feelings
        about adoption 4, 5
        relinquishment 14–16
    interview sample 68–83
    needs summary 194–8
    other support 137–46
    recruitment to study 45–7
    welfare of the child and
        211–16

Contact after Adoption study
19–21, 26
contact applications 11–12
"contact gap" 96–7, 155–6
contact letters see letterbox
(indirect) contact
contact support 4–5, 30, 107–8
costs 178–9
findings 201
relevance/links to other
services 37–9
service use 103, 107–8
social workers' attitudes
38–9
time spent 53–4, 175–6
contact support services 25–6
LA provision 32
VAA provision 32–3
coping with adoption 5, 147–68
measure 52, 147–9, 166–7
outcomes and costs 187–8,
189–90
study results 164–7
costs
case worker diaries 175–7
outcomes and 186–90,
205–6
questionnaire 42
time valuation 54–5
total 180–4
underestimate 6, 54–5, 193
user 178–80
counselling
in contested proceedings 25,
26
costs 53–4, 175–6, 178, 179
emotional support 104–5

provision by VAAs 32–3
rejection of 125–7, 133
unmet needs 131–2
court hearings 9–13
emotional support 106
feelings about 21
criminal records 18, 74, 75

D
delay, avoidance of 9
denial of problems 77–8, 81–2
depression 5–6
at child's removal 72, 85–8
failure to use support 134–5
post-adoption 169, 171
at relinquishment 15
diaries see case worker diaries;
support service use diaries
distress
at child's removal 85–8, 196
post-adoption 169, 171–4
domestic violence 75, 76
drug abuse 18, 72–3
dual connection 49
acceptance of 5, 149–54,
164–5

E
economic analysis 2–3, 43, 53–6
emotional impact
of adoption 157–64
negative indicators 162–4
positive indicators 158–62
emotional support 4–5, 103,
104–6
costs 179–80
findings 201